LIVING BY ZEN

D. T. SUZUKI

D. LITT

late Professor of Buddhist Philosophy in the Otani University, Kyoto

Living by Zen

EDITED BY
CHRISTMAS HUMPHREYS
President of the Buddhist Society
London

RIDER & COMPANY
LONDON

Rider and Company
3 Fitzroy Square, London W1

An imprint of the Hutchinson Publishing Group

London Melbourne Sydney Auckland
Wellington Johannesburg and agencies
throughout the world

First published 1950
This edition 1972
Second impression 1974
Third impression 1977

Printed in Great Britain by The Anchor Press Ltd
and bound by Wm Brendon & Son Ltd
both of Tiptree, Essex

ISBN 0 09 111820 4 (cased)
0 09 111821 2 (paper)

CONTENTS

To the memory of my wife

BEATRICE EARSKINE LANE SUZUKI

EDITOR'S FOREWORD

LIVING BY ZEN was the seventh work by Dr. Suzuki published by Rider and Co. in London in his Collected Works in English, the first edition appearing in 1950.

But the Author was not quite satisfied with the original manuscript, which he sent me for publication in 1949, and in later correspondence made it clear that he was contemplating revision. In 1966, however, he died, and all attempts to find and use such revisions as he may have made have failed. In the circumstances, with the approval of a distinguished Rinzai Zen Roshi, who actually translated the English text for a Japanese edition, I have agreed to a reprint of the first edition as it stands. Readers, however, must bear in mind that the Author was considering, and may have made, improvements in the text, and the work as it stands must be read accordingly.

Its reappearance is overdue, for a whole generation of Zen students in the West has scarcely heard of it. Its genesis makes it different from other works in the Series, as the Author's own Preface makes clear, and in a way it may be regarded as a second introduction to Zen which some may find more helpful than *An Introduction to Zen Buddhism* first published in the Collection in 1947.

Of the Author little need here be said. Born in 1869 of a line of doctors, he was educated in Tokyo University, but soon gave all his time to the study of Zen Buddhism at Engakuji in Kamakura. Under the famous Soyen Shaku Roshi he attained his enlightenment in 1896, just before leaving to work for a period of years with Dr. Paul Carus in Chicago. Back in Japan he dedicated his life to bringing Zen Buddhism into the lives of the people of Japan, writing some thirty books to this end, and in the intervals of frequent visits to Europe adding a further twenty in English.

He wrote with authority. Not only had he studied original works in Sanskrit, Pali, Chinese and Japanese but he had an up-to-date knowledge of Western thought in German and French as well as English, in which he wrote with such charming fluency. He was, however, more than a scholar. Though not a member of any Japanese school of Buddhism he was honoured as an enlightened Buddhist in every temple in Japan.

He died in 1966 at the age of ninety-five, still working, and we shall not in this century know his like again. If the tremendous message of Zen Buddhism is ever integrated into the spiritual life of the West, to the world's advantage, it will be largely due to the work of that great teacher, scholar and man of Zen whom we knew and loved as Daisetz Teitaro Suzuki.

PREFACE

SINCE the end of the war the author has met several young American and English inquirers about the teaching of Zen, whose approach was more or less in the modern scientific spirit. This made him go over anew the ground which he had been accustomed to cover in a somewhat old-fashioned way. Moreover, he has reconsidered to some extent his understanding of Zen in accordance with later experience and reflection. The present book is a partial result of this reconsideration, while he hopes in his future works, if he is allowed to live a few years longer, to give a fuller exposition of Zen.

Mr. Christmas Humphreys has read and revised the MS., for which the author is duly grateful.

DAISETZ TEITARO SUZUKI.

Kamakura, Japan.

I

LIVING BY ZEN

WHAT is meant by "living by Zen"? Are we not all living by Zen, in Zen, and with Zen? Can we ever escape it? However much we may struggle to get away from it or to leap out of it, we are like those small fishes which are kept in the peck; the struggle is of no avail, and it ends in our hurting ourselves badly. From another point of view, "living by Zen" is like putting another head over the one we already have even prior to our birth. What, then, is the use of talking about it?

But it is human nature to ask self-evident questions and often to get inextricably involved in them. It is no doubt the height of stupidity, but it is this very stupidity which opens up a realm of which we have hitherto never suspected the existence. Stupidity is in another word curiosity, and curiosity is what God has implanted in the human spirit. Probably God himself was curious to know himself and created man, and is trying to satisfy his curiosity through man.

However this may be, here is the title of this booklet, *Living by Zen*, and let us see what it means. To do this, we descend from God, from the Life Divine, and make use of the intellect or human consciousness as developed in us, for it is the one thing which characteristically and essentially distinguishes us humans from the rest of creation. The intellect proves itself as a kind of nuisance in more ways than one, but it is a useful instrument in our practical life, and as long as we make judicious use of it we shall derive much benefit from it.

The materialists say that Thought is conditioned by Being and not Being by Thought and that Being with its basis in itself is conditioned by itself. This is very well as far as it goes, but it forgets that without Thought or Consciousness Being is no-Being. Being in point of fact comes into being only when it becomes conscious of itself.

As long as God is content with himself he is non-existent; he must be awakened to something which is not himself, when he is God. God is God when God is not God, yet what is not God must be in himself too. And this—what is not himself—is his own Thought or Consciousness. With this Consciousness he departs from himself and at the same time returns to himself. You cannot say that Thought is by Being and that Being has its basis in itself; you must say that Being is Being because of Thought, which is to say, that Being is Being because Being is not Being.

Zen is the living, Zen is life, and the living is Zen. We do not live by Zen, we are just living it. When we say, however, that we live by Zen, this means that we become conscious of the fact. The importance of this consciousness requires no argument, for is there anything more important in human life than recognizing the Divine in it?

The dog is a dog all the time, and is not aware of his being a dog, of his harbouring the Divine in himself; therefore he cannot transcend himself. He finds bones and jumps at them and eats them; he is thirsty, and drinks water; periodically he chases his female companion, fights with his rivals even to the death. When his life comes to an end, he just expires; he does not lament his fate, he has no regrets, no hopes, no aspirations. Why is all this so? Simply because he is not conscious of his Buddha-nature; he has not been awakened to the truth. He lives Zen just the same, but he does not live by Zen.

It is man alone that can live by Zen as well as live Zen. To live Zen is not enough; we must live by it, which means that we must have the consciousness of living it, although this consciousness is beyond what we generally understand by it. The latter is relative and psychological while the consciousness of living Zen is something qualitatively different from it; it marks the limit of development which the human mind can achieve; it almost approaches divine consciousness.

When God saw the light which came out of his command, he said, "It is good." This appreciation on the part of God is the first awakening of consciousness in the world; in fact the beginning of the world itself. The mere separation of light and darkness does not demonstrate the beginning. The world starts only when there is a mind which appreciates, viz. a mind critically conscious of itself. This is also the eating of "the fruits of the tree which is in the midst of the garden". The eating means "knowing good and evil", appraising the light and darkness, and in this appraisal, in this knowledge, there is the secret of living by Zen.

We all live Zen, non-sentient as well as sentient, but the secret of the living has never been revealed except to human beings. It is their privilege to be in communion with God through this secret knowledge. The secret is no secret when you have it; it is revealed to every being who is endowed with consciousness. "For there is nothing covered that shall not be revealed, and hid that shall not be known."

The living by Zen is more than being merely moral. Morality restrains, binds; Zen releases and brings us out into a wider and freer realm of life. Morality is not creative, and exhausts itself by trying to be other than itself, or rather trying to be itself.

The living by Zen means to remain itself, to be complete by itself, and therefore it is always self-working; it gives out what it has, and never tries or contrives to be other than itself. With Zen every morning is a good morning, every day a fine day, no matter how stormy. Morality always binds itself with the ideas of good and evil, just and unjust, virtuous and unvirtuous, and cannot go beyond them; for if it goes, it will no longer be itself; it is its own nature that it cannot be free and self-independent. Zen is, however, not tied up with any such ideas; it is as free as the bird flying, the fish swimming, and the lilies blooming.

Morality and intellection walk arm in arm, and it is the business of the intellect to divide and hold the one against the other; hence it is up to morality to live by this polarization of good and evil. Morality abides by intellectual judgements. Zen, however, makes or gives no judgements; it takes things as they are. This is, however, not quite exact and may be misleading, for Zen discriminates and gives judgements.

Zen does not ignore the senses, nor intellection, nor morality. What is beautiful is beautiful, good is good, true is true; Zen does not go against the judgements which we commonly make about things as they present themselves for our appreciation. What constitutes Zen is something which Zen adds to all those judgements, and it is when we become aware of this something that we can say that we live by Zen. But the difficulty Zen feels in this connection is its inability to give expression to it adequate to our understanding; so saturated are we with intellectualization.

When Zen gives utterance to itself, it goes against the intellect so as to upset it from its very foundation; the intellect loses its way and stands completely dazed. Zen would declare: The ascetic pure and undefiled enters not into Nirvana, while the Bhikkhu who violates the Precepts falls not into hell, which runs directly contrary to the moralist's idea. Hakuin (1685–1768) comments on this in his characteristic Zen manner:

> The leisurely ants are struggling to carry away the
>   wings of a dead dragon-fly;
> The spring swallows are perching side by side on a
>   willow branch;
> The silk-worm women, pale and tired, stand holding
>   the baskets filled with mulberry-leaves;
> The village urchins are seen with stolen bamboo-shoots
>   creeping through a broken fence.

From the intellectual point of view what connection is there between the statements about the ascetic and the monk and the "commentary" verse of Hakuin? There is none whatever. But Zen finds a great deal of connection, so much indeed that the original statement can be turned into a commentary on Hakuin. When the one is understood the other will yield its meaning.

To comment from the intellectual point of view, the scenes described by Hakuin are those familiar to our daily life; we generally pass them by without finding anything significant. Yet Hakuin depicts them as having something of Zen in them. This means that our daily experiences are, as indeed they are, Zen experiences, but we fail to recognize the fact because we, as intellectuals, lack something which enables us to understand the meaning of the paradoxical statement. "The ascetic pure and undefiled enters not into Nirvana," etc. If so, as long as we remain intellectuals we have no means of escaping from a vicious circle. The living by Zen makes us aware of a mysterious something which escapes intellectual grasp.

Sotoba, one of the greatest literati of the Sung dynasty, who was a student of Zen, has this to say:

> Misty rain on Mount Lu,
> And waves surging in Che Kiang;
> When you have not yet been there,
> Many a regret you have;
> But once there and homeward you wend,
> How matter-of-fact things look!
> Misty rain on Mount Lu,
> And waves surging in Che Kiang.[1]

The misty rain on Mount Lu and the surging waves of the Che Kiang remain the same whether or not you have Zen; as the poet sings, "there is nothing special" before and after your arrival there. The same old world with Zen or without Zen, yet there must be something new in your consciousness, for otherwise you cannot say, "It is all the same."

Living by Zen, then, resolves itself into becoming conscious of "just a little business" which has been in your mind all the time, but of which you failed to take cognizance. "This little business", however, proves itself

[1] *Essays in Zen Buddhism, I,* p. 22.

to be a great business, as it affects the whole tenor of your life.

The moon is shining bright tonight. Objectively we see the same heavenly body which waxes and wanes regularly, and poets have all expressed their different impressions on different occasions. To them the moon is not the same astronomical existence. While Sotoba declares that "there is nothing special" with Mount Lu, there is, spiritually speaking, a great change—revolutionary indeed—which has taken place in the mind of the poet. Being so total and fundamental, he is hardly conscious of the change in the sense he commonly ascribes to it.

When a change is partial there are other things remaining which can be brought out for comparison. In the case of the moon, poetically, romantically impressive, whatever inspiration comes out of it is psychological, and does not leave one's relative consciousness, whereas with Sotoba the sense of "nothing special" has permeated every cell, every fibre, of his existence, and he is no more his old self. Not only he but Mount Lu also is no more the old Lu, its *sat* (Being) has now its *chit* (Thought or Consciousness) as much as its old beholder, Sotoba, and they are finally one in their *ananda* (Bliss). Is this not the greatest event the world can experience?

This little book, then, is devoted to clearing up, if possible, this mysterious event known as Zen, which naturally leads up to describing what is meant by living by Zen.

II

A GENERAL SURVEY

THERE is a school of Buddhism known as Zen. It claims to transmit the quintessence of Buddhist teaching, stating that whatever schools of Buddhism fail to have Zen in them, or whose followers lack an eye of Zen, cannot be called genuinely Buddhist. Zen is, then, according to its devotees, the Alpha and Omega of Buddhism. Buddhism has its beginning in Zen and terminates in Zen. When Zen is taken away from Buddhism the latter ceases to be what it claims to be. This is Zen's pronouncement, and if this be really the case, Zen is not a school of Buddhism but Buddhism itself.

But as history has it, Zen forms a special branch of Buddhist teaching, and has a sectarian institution. While the claim of Zen to be the quintessence of Buddhism will become clearer as we proceed, let us in the meantime treat it as a discipline unique not only in its teaching but in its practical demonstration in our daily life.

I

Zen as characterized by its masters is so utterly, unreasonably unique as to put the uninitiated completely out of wits. See what answers they have given to their anxious inquirers about Zen.

One master said, "Zen is like a pot of boiling oil."

Another, "Monkeys climb the tree, and with their tails holding one another hang from the top."

Another, "It is a piece of broken brick."

Another, "I raise my eyebrows, I move my eyes."

A gardener-monk once approached the master and wanted to be enlightened on Zen. The master said, "Come again when there is nobody around, and I'll tell you what it is." The following day the monk came in again, observed that there was nobody around, and implored him to reveal the secret. The master said, "Come closer to me," and the monk moved forward as told. The master said, "Zen is something that cannot be conveyed by word of mouth."

A similar story is told of Suibi. He was once accosted by Reijun (A.D. 875–919) of Seihei-san, who wanted to know about the secret of Zen as it was brought to China by Bodhi-Dharma. Suibi told him that the secret would be transmitted to him when there was nobody around. When he came again, Suibi dismounted from his chair and took the anxious inquirer down to the bamboo-grove where everything was quiet. Suibi said, pointing to the bamboos, "See how long these are and how short these are."

Strange definitions these, and there is no agreement, even tentatively, among them. There are in fact as many definitions of Zen as there are masters since the beginning of Zen. What about the Buddha, then, who is regarded as the first master? Do they cherish one and the same Buddha?

When a master was asked as to who the Buddha was, he answered, "The cat climbs the post." The disciple confessed his inability to grasp the meaning, and the master said, "If you don't understand, ask the post."

A monk asked, "What is the Buddha?"

Reikwan of Useki-san put his tongue out and showed it to him.

The monk made his bow.

The master said, "Stop that; what did you see to make you bow?"

The monk replied, "It is all due to your kindheartedness that you showed me the Buddha by means of your tongue."

The master said, "Lately I have a sore on the tip of my tongue."

A monk asked Keitsu of Kwaku-san, "Who is the Buddha?"

The master struck him, and the· monk struck the master.

The master said, "There is a reason in your striking me, but there is no such reason in my striking you."

The monk failed to respond, whereupon the master struck him and chased him out of the room.

Yero asked Sekito (A.D. 700–790), "Who is the Buddha?"

Sekito said, "You have no Buddha-nature."

"What about those wiggling creatures, then?"

"They have the Buddha-nature."

"If so, how is it that I, known as Yero, have no Buddha-nature?"

The master said, "Just because you do not give your acknowledgement."

A monk asked Gi-an of Tanka-san, "Who is the Buddha?"

"Who are you?" asked the master.

"If so, there's no difference?"

"Who told you that?"

The post or pillar frequently comes out in Zen *mondo*,[1] for it is one of the common objects in sight in the monastery. A monk asked Sekito, "What is the idea of Bodhi-Dharma's visit to this country?" The master said, "Ask the post." The monk confessed that he did not understand. The master said, "I am worse off in that respect."

From these answers given to the questions, "What is Zen?" and "Who is Buddha?" we can see what kind of teaching Zen is. The way in which Zen conceives of the Buddha does not allow any uniformity among its advocates, and the method to which each master resorts to

[1] The Zen form of question/answer.

make his questioners realize what or who he is tends to
an absurdity beyond human intelligence. Although Zen
may profess to be a form, or even the essence, of Buddhism,
it does not seem to show the slightest inkling of it.

If we are to judge Zen from our common-sense view of
things, we shall find the ground sinking away from under
our feet. Our so-called rationalistic way of thinking has
apparently no use in evaluating the truth or untruth of
Zen. It is altogether beyond the ken of human understanding. All that we can therefore state about Zen
is that its uniqueness lies in its irrationality or its passing beyond our logical comprehension. It is true that
religion has generally something that is not to be
grasped by mere logic, and appeals to a revelation or
acceptance by faith. For instance, the existence of God,
who has created the world out of nothing, is not logically
provable or experientially demonstrable, and is to be
accepted only by faith. But Zen's irrationality does not
seem to be of the same order as the religious irrationality,
so called.

What has Zen, let us ask, which professes to be the
quintessence of Buddhism, to do with the monkey's
climbing the tree or the cat's climbing the post? What has
it to do with one's raising the eyebrows or opening and
shutting the eyes? If we ask the post to explain what the
cat means by climbing it, will or can the post explain it to
us? What do we really gather from these statements
made by Zen masters?

It is true that they talk about Buddha and the truth of
Zen, but their Buddhas evidently do not go further than
the cat and the post, and there is nothing in them which
makes us think of holiness or sacredness or saintliness, the
ideas which we naturally associate with Buddhahood or
the object of religious worship. The cat is not enveloped
with a halo; the post has no resemblance to the Cross.

As to the master's offer to divulge the secret of Zen to
his disciples as soon as they are all alone, can a spiritual
truth be privately communicated from one person to
another? When the disciple came to the master, he was

further requested to come up more closely, as if the secret were to be only whispered by the master.

But no secret reached the disciple's ears except that it was not to be communicated by human speech. Was this really so? Did not the disciple understand the master's command to step forward, and did he not actually move on? Was there a further secret than this? Did not the master betray himself when he commented that there was no secret in Zen that could be communicated by words? And did not the disciple contradict himself when he behaved as if he were altogether ignorant as to the truth of Zen? The whole episode seems to be nothing but a farce. But is it really so? Is there nothing deeply spiritual which is indeed hidden from the intellect but revealed in the disciple's behaviour as well as in the master's speechless communication?

In the second case, where the secret of Zen is again the subject, the master did not say that he could not express it by means of human language. He simply pointed to the bamboos and gave his appraisal as to their length; he did not say a word about the secret message supposed to have been brought to the Middle Kingdom by Bodhi-Dharma. Was any secret revealed here? The bamboos did not apparently convey anything either to Suibi or to Reijun. But, according to *The Record*, the latter is said to have had a glimpse into the truth of Zen. What was it, then? The shorter bamboos are short, the longer bamboos are long, and they remain green throughout the year and stand straight, gracefully swaying in a group as a breeze passes over them.

Baso (–788), one of the greatest Zen masters of the T'ang dynasty, was once accosted by a monk and asked, "Apart from the four propositions and beyond one hundred negations, O Master, be pleased to tell me what is the meaning of Bodhi-Dharma's coming over to this land of ours."

Bodhi-Dharma (–528) is traditionally regarded as the first patriarch of Zen in China; that is to say, he is regarded as the one who first brought the idea of Zen from India to China in the early part of the sixth century. The question, "What is the meaning of his coming to China?" is tantamount to asking, "What is the truth of Zen Buddhism?" Now, the monk who asked this question wished to know if there were anything specifically to be known as the truth of Zen, which is absolutely beyond human understanding. The four propositions are: (1) affirmative, (2) negative, (3) neither affirmative nor negative, and (4) both affirmative and negative. The "one hundred negations", which in fact refers to the one hundred and six negative statements in the *Lankavatara sutra*, means a wholesale negation of all possible statements that can be made of anything.

The monk's question, therefore, amounts to asking about one absolutely ultimate truth, if there could be any such when all is categorically and consistently negated. Is Zen really in possession of such? If so, the monk demanded to have it from the master. In Christian terminology such ultimate truth is God or Godhead. When one sees it or him, one's religious or spiritual quest comes to an end; one's troubled soul finds its final resting place. The monk's question is really no idle question; it flows out of the deepest recesses of his truth-seeking heart. What was Baso's answer? It was this:

"I am tired today and cannot tell it you. Go to Chizo (Chih-tsang) and ask." The monk went to Chizo, who was one of Baso's chief disciples, and repeated the question. Said Chizo, "Why not ask the master himself?" The monk replied, "It is the master himself who directed me to come here and ask you about it." Chizo said: "I have a headache today and cannot tell you anything about it. Go to Brother Kai (Hai) and ask." The monk went to Kai and repeated the question. Said Kai, "As to that, I really have no understanding." The monk finally returned to Baso and reported the whole procedure. The following was Baso's remark, "Chizo's head is white, while Kai's is black."

What we can gather from this Zen "incident" or

"story" (Yin-Yuan) is apparently no more than the master's feeling of tiredness, one of the two disciples having a headache, the other's not understanding, and finally the master's nonchalant comment about the grey hair of the one and the darkness of the other's. All these are trivial incidents of our daily experience, which do not seem to have much to do with such profound subjects as truth or God or reality. And if they are all that Zen could or would give to the earnest seeker of truth after many years of serious inquiries, is Zen really worth studying? The secret message of Bodhi-Dharma who came to China in the sixth century, risking his life over the towering waves of the southern seas—does it not go any further than this?

Whatever this is, we see that the uniqueness of Zen consists not only in its obvious irrationality but also in its most unusual methods of demonstrating its truth. As to irrationality, most religious propositions may be so classed. For instance, take the Christian statement that God sent his only son to save mankind from final condemnation. To say the least, it is highly irrational. God is supposed to be omniscient and omnipotent, and he must have been fully aware of man's destiny when he created him; if so, why did he take the trouble, or had he to take the trouble, of sacrificing his only-begotten son for sinful mankind? Apart from his omniscience, could he not prove his omnipotence by some other means than that of giving his only son to be crucified on the Cross? If God were rational as we humans are, he need not be so irrational as to transform himself into one of us in order to prove his boundless parental love for us. These and many other "irrational" questionings could be raised against the Christian conception of God and his plan of salvation.

The Zen irrationalities may be said to be of another order than those of Christianity, but they are just as irrational so far as illogicality is concerned. Zen says: "I hold a spade in my hands and I am empty-handed. I ride on an ox and I am tramping on foot." Is this not just as illogical and against human experience as when Christians claim that Christ was raised from his grave three days after crucifixion?

There is no doubt that the Zen method of dealing with its subjects is unique in the history of thought. It makes no use of ideas or concepts; it directly appeals to concrete experience. If the monk fails to awaken in himself the consciousness of the truth thus conveyed in the most practical, personal, and lively manner, he has to wait for another opportunity. In the meantime he may go on roaming in the wilderness of abstract thought.

All other religious or spiritual teachings try to prove the truth of their irrationalities by means of deduction or induction, by means of abstraction and rationalization and postulation; but Zen masters refuse to do this. They just let go their "direct action", and give their lessons in a most effectively personal way. If the monk cannot catch it at the moment, the master waits for the next occasion when the monk himself feels an inner urge to approach the master, this time, probably, with another form of question.

When Suiryo approached Baso with the question, "What is the truth of Zen as brought over by Bodhi-Dharma?" the master knocked him down. This rude treatment awakened him to the truth of Zen. When he had restored his balance, he clapped his hands, laughing aloud, and said:

"How strange! All the *samadhis*, all the inexhaustible depths of meaning as told in the *sutras*, are at once revealed at the point of one single hair!" He then made his bows to the master and retired. Later, he used to say, "Since I tasted Baso's kick, I cannot stop laughing." When he was questioned as to the ultimate truth of Buddhism, he simply rubbed his hands and laughed aloud.

In Zen there is a great deal of knocking down, slapping with a hand, and striking with a stick. When a monk is treated in a manner so unexpectedly uncere-monious, he often opens his eye to the truth of Zen, but frequently, it goes without saying, the striking is of no avail and leaves the questioner still in a quandary.

Tokusan (780–866), a great monk of the late T'ang Dynasty, was noted for swinging his staff. His favourite saying was, "No matter what you say, whether 'yes' or 'no', you will get thirty blows just the same." He once gave a sermon in which he said, "If you ask, you are at fault; if you do not, you are also in the wrong." A monk came forward prepared to make his bow, when Tokusan struck him with the staff. The monk protested:

"I was just going to bow to you, and why this blow?"

"If I waited for you to open your mouth, the blow would be no use whatever," said Tokusan.

Kotei was a disciple of Kisu Chijo of Kosan. A monk came to him from Kassan, and when he was performing his ceremonial bows the master struck him. The monk said, "I am here to get your specific instruction, and why this blow, Master?" So saying, he made his bows again. The master gave him another blow and drove him out of the monastery.

The monk came back to Kassan, to whom he made a full report of his interview with Kotei. Kassan said, "Do you understand Kotei?" "No, Master, I do not," said the monk. Thereupon Kassan remarked, "It was fortunate that you did not; if you did, that would turn me dumb."

When Chosa was enjoying the moon with one of his brother monks, Kyosan of the ninth century, the latter remarked, "Everyone has this, and it is a pity that he fails to make full use of it." Said Chosa, "May I get you to make use of it?" Kyosan replied, "You try, O Brother monk." Whereupon, Chosa gave Kyosan a hard kick which knocked him down. Rising from the ground, said Kyosan, "O my Brother monk, you are not really like a wild tiger."

Zen literature recounts quite a number of such records, which may frighten away some of the uninitiated. They may think Zen to be just a form of discipline charged with rudeness and irrationality and probably with much that is sheer nonsense. Zen's claim to be the essence of Buddhist teaching may be mere bragging. This criticism may be right if the critic's insight cannot go deeper than superficiality. But the historical fact is that Zen has been flourishing ever since its establishment in China more than one thousand years ago, and that it is still in Japan an active spiritual force in the formation of her culture. The conclusion one may draw from this is that after all there may be something vital in Zen which appeals directly to our deeper spiritual experiences.

II

Another unique factor in the Zen method of teaching is what is known as *mondo*. The disciple asks a question (*mon*) and the master answers (*to* or *do*), but sometimes this is reversed; and the answer is not always given in words. For this questioning and answering is carried on in the region of concrete thinking, and not in that of abstraction and ratiocination. There is no lengthy exchange of words between master and disciple, no discursive argument. The mondo generally stops with the master's pithy, epigrammatic statement, or his physical display of force, and never leads to a serial development of logical subtleties. If the disciple should fail to comprehend the master at once, he beats a retreat, and that is the finish of the personal interview.

Zen never commits itself to conceptualization; it lives in aesthetic or intuitive apprehension, and its truth is always demonstrated by means of personal contact, which is the signification of mondo. The knocking down, or the slapping of the face, or other various acts of "rudeness" or violence, are the natural outcome of the personal contact. It may appear strange that the understanding of Zen issues out of these deeds, but as long as Zen is not based on logical reasoning and conceptual persuasion, its understanding must come from personal experience itself, and it must be understood that by personal experience is meant not only the experience of the sense-world but that of events taking place in one's psychological realm.

Rinzai (–867) once gave a sermon to the following effect: "There is one true man without a title on the mass of red-coloured flesh; he comes out and goes in through your sense-gates. If you have not yet borne witness to him, look, look!"

A monk came forward and asked, "Who is this true man without a title?"

Rinzai came down from his chair and taking hold of his chest demanded, "Speak, speak!"

The monk hesitated, whereupon letting him go exclaimed, "What kind of dirt scraper is this true man without a title!" So saying, Rinzai went back to his room.

The idea of "one true man without a title" is clear enough, general enough; but when a witness to his presence in every one of us is demanded, Rinzai resorts not to verbosity but to a direct personal encounter. The questioner is taken to task to give his existential testimony, as it were. No abstract dialectics here, but a fact of living experience full of flesh and blood. When Rinzai could not have it from the monk whose mind was working on the plane of intellectual elaboration, he pushed him away and called him an old dirt-scraper. "The one true man with no title" turned out to be an ignominious piece of wood. This is the fate of the rationalist. And it is only in the hands of the Zen master that "the blade of an insignificant grass by the roadside is made to shine out in the golden colour of the Buddha sixteen feet high". Rinzai, that is, Zen demands this of every one of us.

In this respect, Christ may be said to belong to the Zen school of Buddhism when he declares that "Except ye eat the flesh of the son of man, and drink his blood, ye have no life in you" (John vi, 53). Whatever the philosopher or spiritualist may say about our bodily existence, we are hungry when we do not eat, we are thirsty when there is not enough to drink—such are concrete facts of human experience. We are all made of flesh and blood and it is in these that the truth of Zen sees the light.

Therefore, the Zen master describes Zen to be like a pot of boiling oil. This is the actual experience of every student of Zen, for he has to dip his fingers right into it and taste it to his heart's content. Again, Zen is described as a life of "seven trippings and eight tumblings", which means a state of indescribable confusion; the idea is that Zen is attained only after going through a series of mental and spiritual crises. To apprehend the truth of Zen is no easy intellectual gymnastics. One has to eat one's own flesh and drink one's own blood.

By way of commentary, let me add a few words here. When it is said that the spiritual life issues out of eating Christ's flesh and drinking his blood, it may sound grossly materialistic, but from the Zen point of view it is a great mistake to make distinction between mind and body, and to take them as irrevocably differentiated the one from the other. This dualistic view of reality has been a great stumbling-block to our right understanding of the spiritual truth.

The following remarks may help the reader to clarify the Zen point of view in regard to an advaitistic[1] conception of reality. When Chosha, a disciple of Nansen (748–834), was asked, "What is the Buddha?" he replied, "He is no other than this corporeal body of ours." It is significant that Chosha has here the corporeal body (*rupakaya*) which is identified with Buddha, and not the mind or soul or spirit which we popularly hold up for identification in such cases. Buddhahood is not generally associated with corporeality; it is something quite apart from our bodily presence which we usually relegate to a lower order of existence. Chosha has put his finger on the most vulnerable spot in our common-sense rationalism. One of the objects of Zen training is to crush the dualistic idea of mind and body. The master is emphatic about this. The following are quoted from the *Transmission* of the Lamp (fas. X):

[1] Non-dualistic.

Here stands no wall of obstruction that resists your
     making way,
There is no vacuum that permits your free passage:
When your understanding reaches this point,
Mind and body recover their primary self-identity.[1]
The Buddha-nature is manifest in a most conspicuous
     way.
It is only those who tarry with the nature that fail to
     see it:
When we are enlightened as to the selflessness of all
     beings,
What difference is there between my face and Buddha's
     face?

Somebody asked Chosha, "How can we transform
mountains, rivers, and the great earth, and reduce them
into this Self?"

Replied the master, "How can we transform this Self
and turn it into mountains, rivers, and the great earth?"

The monk failed to understand, whereupon the master
said, "This town on the south side of the Lake is a good
site for the people to get settled, for here rice is cheap, fuel
abundant, neighbours friendly."

Then he gave the following *gatha*:

Who is it that asks about the transforming of mountains
     and rivers?
What do mountains and rivers turn into?
Here is perfect interfusion, and no bifurcation:
The Dharma-nature knows nowhere to reduce itself.

The bifurcation here referred to is between Dharma-
nature and rivers and mountains and great earth and all
other corporealities, between mind and body, between the
"wall of obstruction" and the "emptiness of a vacuum",
between Buddha-nature and those whose minds are not
yet concept-free. The bifurcation is the work of the
intellect, and inasmuch as we cannot get along in our

[1] "The wall of obstruction" is the body or matter which resists, and "the
emptiness of vacuum" refers to mind or "the universal". Chosha denies the
dualistic conception of reality.

practical life without resorting to it, we make full use of it, but we must not let it intrude into our spiritual realm.

Yakusan (751–834) was once asked by his master Baso, "How are you getting along these days?" Yakusan answered, "The skin is left to itself to fall off, baring the one true substance only." The "one true substance" or Reality, however, is not to be understood in the sense of a kernel or hypostasis or thing-in-itself existing apart from what is known as appearance or phenomenality. It is not an object of intellectual perception to be distinguished as this or that. It is that which remains behind (though we do not like to use this kind of expression) when all the outer skin or casing falls off. This is not to be understood on the plane of intellection. It is symbolic and to be spiritually interpreted; it is the feeling one has while going through what we may call, for lack of proper terminology, Zen experience or satori.

While Zen emphatically asserts the all-importance of the personal contact, it does not ignore the privilege of conceptualization granted only to the human mind; that is to say, Zen will also resort to verbalism. But what distinguishes Zen conspicuously from other spiritual teachings is its assuming perfect mastery over words or concepts. Instead of becoming a slave to them, it is aware of the role they play in human experience, and assigns them to the place to which they properly belong.

Man is *homo sapiens* and also *homo faber*; but the greatest danger he is apt to court in his capacity as *homo faber* is that he becomes a slave to his own creations. Man makes many tools and uses them effectively in various fields of his activity, but he is always exposing himself to the tyranny of the tools he has made. The result is that he is no more master of himself, but an abject slave to his surroundings, and the worst thing is that he is not conscious of this fact.

This is specially noticeable in the realm of thought. He has created many valuable concepts by which he has learnt to handle realities. But he now takes concepts for realities, thought for experience, system for life. He forgets that concepts are his own creations, and by no means exhaust reality. Zen is fully conscious of this, and all its mondo are directed towards casting off the false mask of conceptualization. It is for this reason that Zen looks so irrational, and smudges our common-sense picture of the world.

When Hokoji of the eighth century asked Baso regarding the "companionless one in the ten thousand things", Baso said, "Drink up in one draught all the waters in the West Lake and I will tell you what he is."

Someone asked Koboku, a disciple of Kyosan Yejaku of the ninth century, "What is right hearing?" The master said, "It is not heard by the ears." "What do you mean, master?" The master's reply in the form of a counter-question was, "Do you hear now?"

What do we gather from such mondo? In the first one an impossibility is asked, for how could one drink up the whole lake in one draught? As far as our common-sense experience goes, no such feats are possible. But even if this could be achieved, what has the deed to do with "the companionless one" which apparently corresponds to our notion of the Absolute? Did the master mean that the Absolute could be apprehended by reversing the order of our everyday experience? Or does the drinking-up of the whole lake merely symbolize the thorough-going negation of our ordinary world of realities? Is it considered that the Absolute is thus reachable? Evidently the master had no such intellectual contrivance.

His demand to drink up the whole lake had nothing of ratiocination behind it. He simply blurted it out as casually as he would say, "Have a cup of tea." "The companionless one" was no abstract notion for Baso. It was just as concrete a being as anything else one sees about. When Joshu (878–897) was asked what the essence of Buddhism is, he said, "The cedar tree in the courtyard." The answer came from him quite naturally, he had no intellectual scruple or machination behind it.

Baso's reference, too, to the lake was just as spontaneous as in the case of Joshu.

As regards the above-cited mondo on "the true hearing", its procedure assumes a somewhat different aspect from the one on the lake. Its suggestion of negativism is more apparent. When the master says that the true hearing does not come in by means of an ear, he might have had in his mind the logic of negation as expounded in the *Prajna Paramita Sutras*. For, according to them, Prajna is not Prajna and for this reason Prajna is Prajna. Was Koboku thinking of this when he said that the true hearing is not to hear through the ears?

If he was he is no Zen master, for in the world of Zen there is no abstraction, no dialectic, no intellectual deliberation. When somebody strikes a bell, he hears it right away and says without hesitation, "I hear the bell." When he sees a flower he says in the same way, "I see the flower." He does not say this after meditating or cogitating on Prajna philosophy. His experiences are always straightforward, based on intuition or aesthetic apprehension, and do not reflect anything of philosophizing. Therefore, when Koboku found his questioner did not understand what he meant, he immediately gave out this, "You now hear, do you not?" This shows conclusively that Koboku's mind has never wandered away from the immediacy of the sense-world, though his sense-world is penetrated through with Zen insight.

III

All religious experience is unique in the sense that it refuses to be explained away by common-sense logic, and contains in it facts which suggest the presence in our consciousness of something irresolvable to ratiocination, which naturally leads to the idea of faith or revelation or supernaturalism. In this sense, Zen is unique as much as any other religious experience; but what makes Zen unique in a most specific sense is its methodology, which, besides being made up of a series of paradoxes and contradictions and irrationalities, operates in intimate connection with our daily experiences.

In most religious teaching we are told to believe in God, or some being standing above or beside us, for it is from him that something wondrous will follow. Zen reverses this order, and presents us first with wonderful things concretely related to our sense-world, and through them expects us to reach their source. It declares that black is white and white is black, that waters do not flow, but the bridge does, that the Zen master's staff is at once straight and not straight, that the wooden horse neighs and the girl in marble dances.

When such expressions are unexpectedly thrust before us we lose our intellectual balance and do not know what to make of them. Taking advantage of this, the masters press on us to extract if possible anything that amounts to an answer. Neither an affirmation nor a negation will satisfy them. "Do not say it is a stick, nor say it is not a stick, but speak, speak!" "Speak, speak!" means "say something" or "do something". If you know the way to get out of the dilemma, you know how to give it an expression which makes the Zen master nod in approval.

It may not be quite correct to state that Zen is an experience and that its uniqueness consists in the uniqueness of this experience. The correct statement is that in Zen there is no subject that experiences, nor is there any object that is experienced. When we talk in our common parlance about experience, it refers to a part of our existence and there is naturally that which experiences and that which is experienced.

Zen is not this kind of experience; it is not a partial, fragmentary experience. The Zen experience so-called involves the whole being—that which makes one what one is—which goes through a total transformation. And in this total transformation nothing is left that reminds one of the old thing. Apparently the "I" is not changed; existentially it has the same old organs of sense, the old intellect and feeling, and the world where this "I" is placed has the same old references: the river flows, the ocean surges, the mountain towers, the birds sing, the flowers bloom, the animals romp around. Yet with all these old familiar happenings about me, the "I" is not the same "I", nor is the world the same world. A total transformation has taken place somewhere; it cannot be called an experience. Experience is psychological, while the transformation Zen refers to is not merely psychological; it may be termed metaphysical or existential, which is more than psychological. Zen has its psychological aspect no doubt, but it goes further. If Zen stops at psychology, its references to the "dancing of the goddess in marble" or to the "neighing of the wooden horse" will be a case of psychiatrical study.

What may be designated as a total existential transformation is, then, what is known as Zen "experience", and it is from this "unique" point of view that the whole literature of Zen is to be scanned and given interpretation.

When a master was asked "What is the primary[1] face?" he closed his eyes and put out his tongue, and then opened his eyes and put out his tongue again. The monk remarked, "I see primarily there is a variety of faces." The master said, "What did you see just now?" The monk made no answer.

This mondo does not seem to be of any consequence as far as the sticking out of the tongue and the closing and opening of the eyes are concerned; indeed they are childish tricks, amusing no doubt, but could there be any sense deserving a serious consideration on the part of the Zen student? The problem of the original face is fraught with grave significance; it cannot be disposed of as a mere childish entertainment, however innocent and amusing; it is a serious subject for philosophical study, requiring many years of laborious thinking.

What is it, then, that makes the Zen master handle

[1] Or "original". "The original face" is the one we have even prior to our birth. We can say that this is also the face of Christ who "is even before Abraham was". It is one of the koan often given to the beginner.

such intensely absorbing subjects with such apparent levity and indifference? Instead of appealing to abstraction and conceptualism, he passes over them light-heartedly; there must be something in him which connects it to the depths of reality. The twinkling of the eyes, the lifting of a finger or the thrusting out of the tongue may appear trivialities, but in the eyes of the Zen master they are just as grave, serious, and tremendous as the shaking of the earth or the bursting of the heavenly bodies. A mysterious light flashes in the sky and tens of thousands of human lives instantly vanish out of existence. This is a serious event compelling every thoughtful person of the world to ponder in a most deliberate fashion; there is no comparison between this and the twinkling of the eyes as far as their physical and moral consequences are involved. But from the Zen point of view, rooted in reality itself, the one as much as the other is like whisking a particle of dust from the surface of the desk.

Evidently there is a world where human psychology and the human sense of morality and goodness do not enter, where God alone sits quietly and contemplates all human passions, sufferings, and follies; and it is the mystery of mysteries that this world is not apart from the world where we mortals live and die like dewdrops. Zen masters too are here, but what distinguishes them from the rest of us is that they are cognizant of the fact. Their acts, their sayings, are constantly referred to it, and what appears nonsensical to us thereby gains significance.

The following mondo may shed light on the statements so far made:

Isan (771–853) asked Ungan, "Where is the seat of Bodhi (enlightenment)?"

Ungan said, "Non-action (*asamskrita*) is the seat."

Ungan now turned to Isan and asked him to give his view. Isan answered, "Emptiness (or nothingness or *sunyata*) is the seat."

Ungan then asked Dogo, "What is your view?"

Dogo replied: "Wanting to sit, he is allowed to sit; wanting to lie down, he is allowed to lie down. There is, however, one who neither sits nor lies down. Speak quick, speak quick!"

With this, Isan was satisfied.

Another time Isan asked Dogo, "Where have you been?"

Dogo said, "I have been seeing the sick."

"How many are sick?"

"Some[1] are sick, some are not."

"The one who is not sick—is he not Chi[2] the monk himself?"

"Sick or not sick—that does not at all concern him. Speak quick, speak quick!"

"Even when you can speak quick, that has nothing to do with him." This was Isan's conclusion.

A monk asked, "How do we deal with this present moment?"

Dogo Sochi said, "Do not turn your head around even when thousands of people are calling to you; when you can do this, there is some correspondence."

"What will take place when a fire suddenly breaks out?"

"It sets the great earth on fire."

Dogo Sochi now asked the monk, "When the stars and flames are annihilated, what do you call a fire?"

The monk said, "That is no fire."

There was another who asked the master, "Do you see a fire?"

The master said, "Yes, I see a fire."

"Where is this seeing from?"

The master demanded, "Apart from your sitting and lying, walking and staying, you propose a question."

These mondo purpose to have our eyes fixed upon the seat of satori (enlightenment), "which (or who) neither

---

[1] The Chinese, as well as the Japanese, generally makes no distinction in numbers.

[2] Chi or Sochi was Dogo's name.

sits nor lies", upon "the one who is not at all concerned with sickness and no-sickness", or upon "the fire that sets the whole universe in flames and yet is above both seeing and being seen", upon "the one who proposes a question though he is that which neither walks nor stands, neither lies nor sits". When your eyes have once caught a glimpse of this mysterious thing, you never remain dumb, you can speak right out what "fire" it is—the fire that reduces the entire universe into ashes and yet upholds mountains as mountains, rivers as rivers, stars as stars.

"Speak" (*tao*) or "speak quick" (*su tao*) or "say one word" (*tao i chu*) is one of the favourite terms used by Zen masters, and is significant in many ways; for by this they demand us to show proof that we have really gone beyond good and bad, yes and no, this and that. But we must remember, as we shall see later, that this going beyond is not really just going out of dualistic thinking, but appraising this way of thinking from the absolute point of view, in a sense *sub specie eternitatis*. Zen wants us to be factual, not conceptual, witnesses of this viewpoint. It is for this reason that the terms Zen uses in its exposition or interpretation or communication are in most cases concrete, and belong to the categories of our ordinary experience.

Shall we say that what makes Zen unique in our spiritual experience consists in its way of handling abstract subjects in a concrete, natural, realistic, though often quite unrealistic, manner, without appealing to reasoning and postulation? Most religious truths are expressed paradoxically, and Zen does this too. But what distinguishes Zen is its plain-speaking, its dealing with them in a matter-of-fact manner as if they were matters not at all transcending our everyday experience.

However sketchy and imperfect, these considerations, I hope, will help our readers to have a general idea as to what Zen is, or to see what are some of the chief constituents of its uniqueness. From these, however, it ought not to be inferred that living by Zen has something unique or extraordinary about it, for it is, on the contrary, a most ordinary thing, not at all differentiated from the rest of the world. In fact to be ordinary is Zen, and to be contrary is not Zen; your daily life, however much you have Zen, is not to deviate from that of your neighbours. If there is any deviation, it must be in your inner life, which, as will be explained later, has three characteristics: *sat*, *chit*, and *ananda*. *Sat* is Being or Reality, *chit* is Thought or Self-Consciousness which is not conscious of itself, and *ananda* is Bliss.

APPENDIX

Hoping that some more typically Zen mondo may help the reader to have a glimpse into the methodology resorted to by Zen masters, and also into the essentials of the Zen teaching, the following are quoted from *The Transmission of the Lamp*:

1. When an Osho, whose name is unknown, first interviewed Kinrin Kakwan, the latter asked, "What is the Way?"

The Osho replied, "No use inserting a wedge into empty space."

Kakwan said, "Space itself is the wedge."

The Osho struck Kakwan. But Kakwan took hold of the Osho and said: "Don't strike me so. You may later strike others unreasonably."

The Osho was satisfied.

2. Joshu saw Fuyo and Fuyo said: "Old man, what makes you go about so much? You are really old enough to get settled somewhere."

"Where shall I get settled?"

"There is an old temple lot at the foot of this mountain."

"Why don't you make it your own?"

Later Joshu came to Shuyu-san and the presiding

Osho said: "Old man, what makes you go about so much? You are really old enough to get settled somewhere."

"Where shall I get settled?"

"There is an old temple lot at the foot of this mountain."

"Why don't you make it your own?"

Later Joshu came to Shuyu-san and the presiding Osho said: "Old man, what makes you go about so much? You are really old enough to get settled somewhere."

"Where shall I get settled?"

"Old man, are you so old as not to know where?"

Joshu remarked, "I have been a horse-trainer for the last thirty years, and today am kicked by an ass."

3. A monk asked Seizan Osho of So-shu (Su-chou):

"I am not going to ask you about the three Vehicles or about the Twelve divisions of the Scripture, but I wish to know what is the true meaning of the First Patriarch's coming from the West."

The Osho raised his *hossu* and showed it to him. The monk left the Osho without bowing. Later he came to Seppo. Seppo asked, "Where do you come from?"

The monk said, "I come from Setsuchu."

Seppo: "Where did you pass the summer session?"

"With Seizan of So-shu."

"Is the Osho doing well?"

"He was very well when I last left him."

"Why did you not stay with him?"

"Because I have not been able to get enlightened about Buddhism."

"What is the matter?"

The monk then told him about the interview he had had with the Osho.

Seppo said, "Why did you not agree with him?"

"Because it is just a *kyo* (externality)."[1]

[1] *Kyo* literally means "boundary", "limits", probably from the Sanskrit *gocara*. It is the external world contrasted to person (*nin*), subjectivity.

Seppo: "Do you see the houses and people, men and women living in the city of So-shu?"

"Yes, I see them."

"Do you see the plants and woods along the roadside?"

"Yes, I see them."

"Houses and people, men and women, the earth and the trees and lakes—are they not all the *kyo*? Do you agree to this?"

"Yes, I do."

Seppo then said, "Why do you not then approve of the Osho's raising the *hossu*?"

The monk said, bowing down: "I am sorry for my thoughtless remarks. Please have mercy on me."

Seppo said, "All the universe is this eye, and where do you want to lay yourself down?"

The monk remained silent.

4. When Joshu was with Nansen, he asked, "What is the Way?"

Nansen: "Your everyday mind—this is the Way."

Joshu: "Do we need any special conducting or not?"

Nansen replied, "No, when we turn towards it, we turn away from it."

"But if we do not (need any special conducting), how do we find the Way?"

Nansen: "The Way transcends both knowledge and no-knowledge. Knowledge is illusion, no-knowledge is indifference. When you really arrive at the point where not a shadow of doubt is possible, it is like vastness of space, empty and infinitely expanding. You have no way either to affirm or to negate."

This is said to have led Joshu to a spiritual awareness.

5. Joshu once asked, "Where would one who knows find his final place of rest?"

Nansen said, "He becomes an ox in one of the farmhouses at the foot of the mountain."

Joshu: "I am grateful for your direction."

Nansen: "Last night at midnight the moon shone through the windows."

6. Shiko Risho of Kushu appeared before the Sodo (monk's quarters) in the middle of the night and cried out, "Burglar!"

The monks ran about wildly. The master took hold of a monk at the back entrance and called out loudly to the head monk, "I have the burglar, monitor!" The monk-suspect said, "O master, I am not the burglar!" The master said, "That is all right, but you do not acknowledge it."

7. When Shiso was studying Zen under Nansen, he asked: "(I am told that) the *mani*-stone is not known to man; it is kept hidden in the womb of Tathagatahood. What is this womb of Tathagatahood?"

Nansen said, "The womb is that which moves along with you."

"What is that which does not move?"

"The womb is that too."

"What is the *mani*-stone?"

Nansen called out, "Shiso!"

He replied, "Yes, Master."

Nansen said, "Be gone, you don't understand my words."

Shiso now had his satori.

8. Keishu, the monk, asked Ungo-chi about the meaning of the dictum considered to characterize the teaching of Zen. "By seeing into one's own Nature (or Being) one becomes a Buddha."

Ungo-chi gave this answer: "The Nature is primarily pure, absolutely tranquil, altogether free from disturb-ances, does not belong to the category of being and non-being, purity and defilement, longness and shortness, attachment and detachment; it is serenity itself. When one has a clear insight of it, one is said to have seen into one's own Nature. The Nature is the Buddha, and the Buddha is the Nature. Hence seeing into the Nature is becoming the Buddha."

The monk: "If the Nature is pure in essence and has no attribute, either being or non-being, how can there be any seeing at all?"

Chi: "Though there is the seeing, there is nothing seen."

Monk: "If there is nothing seen, how can there be any seeing?"

Chi: "The seeing itself is not."

Monk: "In this kind of seeing, whose seeing is it?"

Chi: "There is no seer either."

Monk: "Where are we then?"

Chi: "Do you know that the idea of being is the product of false thinking? Because of this there is subject and object, which we call an error. When there is a seeing (dualistically conceived), difference of opinion arises, and one falls into birth-and-death. It is not so with the one who has a clear seeing. He sees all day, and yet he sees nothing. The seeing has neither substance nor manifestation; action and reaction are both lacking in it; therefore it is called seeing into the Nature."

Monk: "Is the Nature present everywhere?"

Chi: "Yes, there is nowhere it is not present."

Monk: "Are plain-minded people supplied with it also?"

Chi: "I have already said that there is nowhere the Nature is not present, and why not in the plain-minded people too?"

Monk: "Why is it, then, that while Buddhas and Bodhisattvas are not bound up by birth-and-death, plain ordinary people are to undergo its bondage? Does this not go against the omnipresence?"

Chi: "The trouble is that the latter imagine, in spite of the Nature's being absolutely pure, the opposition of action and reaction in it, and this makes them fall into birth-and-death. Buddhas and great souls are fully cognizant of the truth that there is no distinction between being and non-being in the purity of the Nature, and therefore action and reaction does not take place."

Monk: "If so, some are completed,[1] while others are not?"

Chi: "There is no completion to talk about, how much less the completed one!"

Monk: "What is the ultimate truth?"

Chi: "To state briefly, you should think of this: in the Nature absolutely pure there are neither plain-minded people nor wise men, neither the completed nor the not-completed. The plain-minded or the wise—they are names. When your understanding is based on names, you fall into birth-and-death. When you know that names are provisional and have no reality, you find that there are no personalities corresponding to names."

Chi said again: "This is the ultimate position we come to, and if we here say 'I am the completed one but they are not,' we commit a great error. And another great error is to think that in the seeing there is (the distinction of) pure and defiled, common and wise. But if we take the view that there are no differences of understanding between the common people and the wise, this will be ignoring the law of causation. Further, it is a great error to consider that in the absolutely pure Nature there is a place for abiding.

"It is great error, too, to hold that this is not a place for abiding. While there is nothing moving and disturbing in the absolutely pure Nature, it is furnished with measures and activities which never cease to work, and whereby love and compassion are set to work. Where these workings take place there is the fulfilment of the absolutely pure Nature. This is the seeing into one's Nature and becoming the Buddha."

9. Gensha Shibi (834–908) of Fukushu was one of the chief disciples of Seppo. One day he took up a turnip and asked a monk:

"This is a turnip, and any remark to make?"

[1] Meaning "enlightened" or "attaining satori".

There were over one hundred monks, and many responded to the master's challenge, but none pleased him. Later Gensho appeared and said, "I'll eat, master."

"What will you eat?" asked Gensha.

"I'll eat the turnip," said Gensho.

This satisfied Gensha very much, who said, "You know it, you know it." The master continued: "I have been asking you for some time what you will eat. But you have failed to understand me and have tried to turn it simply into a subject for discourse. If you keep on like this there will be no end to it. I hasten to say this to you now: When you receive a word, you should know its ultimate meaning. What you eat, you eat; when you work, you work; nothing is plainer than this; black is black, white is white. I am consistently reminding you of this: No hesitancy in telling black from white and white from black.

"Don't be so dull-brained; that will never do. Through twelve hours of the day I have not missed a minute telling you all about it, and yet you have not improved. Don't think you have happily found a word to express the situation. Even when you do, it is just a matter of ordinary occurrence, nothing unusual. But when you can go on like this you are quite free, skipping and jumping, high and low, and there is no need here of your learning how to step."

A monk who came back from the mountain produced a turnip and said to the Master Gensha, "O master, what do you say to this?"

Gensha said, "You just eat it."

"What about the turnip that is eaten up?" asked the monk.

"You are filled, I am filled." This was the master's reply.

10. One of Gensha's sermons ran thus: "O Brethren, the one is not the one; the many is not the many. Do you understand? When you say you do not, all right, you do not. When you say you do not, all right, you do not. O

Brethren, what kind of satori have you had? When you have one, things are, just the same, such as they are. When you say you have none, things are, just the same, such as they are. What reason is there that makes (Zen) so difficult to understand? Seeing, feeling, and knowing—the senses are there unchanged. O Brethren, when you talk thus, what do you think they are meant to express? Let it be known to you all unmistakably, that things are finally of absolute oneness."

A monk asked: "What is the One?"

G.: "The many."

M.: "What is the many?"

G.: "The One!"

M.: "What is the Buddha-mind?"

G.: "The mind of sentient beings."

M.: "What is the mind of sentient beings?"

G.: "The Buddha-mind."

M.: "What is my Self?"

G.: "What do you want to do with Self?"

M.: "Am I not just facing you?"

G.: "I have never seen you."

M.: "Who is the right master of this Gensha Monastery?"

G.: "You are he, and I am the guest."

M.: "Why so?"

G.: "What do you ask?"

III

SATORI

I

To understand Zen, it is essential to have an experience known as Satori, for without this one can have no insight into the truth of Zen, which, as we have already seen, is generally paradoxically expressed:

"When snow covers all the mountains white, why is one left uncovered (literally, not white)?"

"The ascetic, pure in heart, does not enter Nirvana (i.e. Paradise); the monk violating the Precepts does not fall into Hell."

"What I know, you do not know; what you know, I know all."

"While the post is moving around all day, how is it that I do not know?"

"How is it that a man of great strength cannot lift his legs?"

All these statements defy being fitted into the frame of logical reasonableness. To make them intelligible satori is needed. They are in fact purposely set forth by Zen masters to confuse those minds whose field of operation cannot go beyond our everyday common-sense experience. When satori is attained the irrationalities cease to be such; they fall back on the level of logic and commonsense. The hunter is said not to know the mountains because he is right in them. He has to be up in the air to see the whole range of the undulations.

Satori achieves this feat; it detaches a man from his environment, and makes him survey the entire field. But this does not mean that satori keeps him away from the field where it operates. This is a dualistic way of interpreting satori, for a genuine satori is at once transcendent

and imminent. It becomes really operative at the point
where subject is object and object is subject. Or we can
say that unless this identity is effected there is no satori.
In satori what is imminent is transcendent and what is
transcendent is imminent. The hunter is at once out of the
mountains and in them, for he has never gone one step
away from them.

We must remember, however, that satori is not a mere
intellectual discipline; nor is it a kind of dialectic whereby
contradictoriness becomes logically tenable and turns
into a reasonable proposition. Satori is existential and not
dialectical, as Kierkegaard may say. It does not work
with logical formulas and abstractions. It is a concrete
fact in itself. When it states that the waters do not flow
but the bridge does, it is, to men of satori, not a paradox
but a direct statement of their living existential experience. Kierkegaard says that faith is an existential leap.
So is satori. Faith has a Christian ring, while satori is
specifically Zen. In my view both are experientially
identifiable.

What is given us primarily, immediately, is a continuum which is not divisible into atoms; but as we
"experience" it, it divides itself into an infinity of atoms.
This is due to our sense limitations and to the construction
of consciousness. We do not ordinarily reflect on this fact
and go on with our daily life, taking sensual-intellectual
facts of experience for finalities. Those who reflect, however, build up a world of concepts, and postulate a continuum. But as this is the result of intellectual deliberation
the continuum is not apprehended as such by most of us.

To us, therefore, God is not an object of immediate
experience. He is inferred by logical process. He is thought
of, he is not seen. From thinking to seeing is not a continuous process, it is a leap. For however much we
multiply our atomic experiences of parts, no continuum
as a concrete whole will be experienced. The concrete
whole is to be intuited as such. The whole is not to be
apprehended by accumulations; a whole thus arrived at
is no more than parts added, and however far we may

carry this addition it goes on *ad infinitum*. An all-embracing whole must be directly grasped as a whole complete in itself. But if it is grasped in the way in which parts, atomic parts, are grasped, it ceases to be a whole, it turns to be a part of the whole which, as an infinitely expansible totality, for ever eludes our prehension, which is postulationally conditioned.

Therefore, the continuum, undivided, indivisible, infinitely cumulative, and yet a concrete object of apprehension, cannot belong to the world of particulars. It belongs to another order of existence; it constitutes a world by itself, and it is attainable only by transcending our everyday experience of sense-intellect, that is, by an existential leap. This is satori.

It is thus seen that satori is the apprehending of the continuum as such, as not subject to differentiation and determination. But the continuum thus apprehended as the object, as it were, of satori experience ought not to be judged as standing against particular objects of our daily experience. When this way of thinking is cherished, satori is no more satori; it turns to be one of sense-experiences, and creates a new continuum over the one we already have, and we shall have to repeat this process indefinitely.

Another important thing to remember is that satori takes in the continuum not only as undifferentiated and undeterminated but as infinitely divided and determinated. This means that satori is never in conflict with the world of sense-intellect, it never negates its experiences. When it declares that the spade is in my hands and yet I am empty-handed, it does not mean to contradict the fact of the spade's actually being in the hands, but it only means that each single fact of experience is to be related to the totality of things, for thereby it gains for the first time its meaning.

The negating by satori of our everyday facts of experience is to make us thereby realize that God's hands are also holding the spade. When satori makes us conscious of the spade being held in God's hands and not in my hands which I imagine to be my own, each movement I perform becomes directly connected with the one who is more than myself, and reflects his will. Hence the Christian saying, "Let thy will be done, not mine." Christians are more ethical and do not speak about negating our common-sense experience. Satori in this respect reflects the general characteristic of Buddhist teaching, especially that of Prajna philosophy.

The Prajna begins its thinking with denying everything; the idea, however, is not to build up a system of philosophy, but to free us from all our egoistic impulses and the idea of permanency, for these are the source of human miseries, are not intellectually tenable and are spiritually altogether unsound. They are the outgrowth of Ignorance (*avidya*), declares the Buddha. Satori is enlightenment (*sambodhi*), just the opposite of ignorance and darkness. Enlightenment consists in spiritually elucidating facts of experience and not in denying or abnegating them. The light whereby satori illuminates the continuum also illuminates the world of divisions and multitudes. This is the meaning of the Buddhist dictum: *Shabetsu* (difference) and *Byodo* (sameness) are identical.

That "a seed of mustard conceals Mount Sumeru", or that "in a handful of water scooped up in my palm the mermaids are seen dancing to their hearts' content", may sound too extravagant for a serious consideration by philosophically-minded people. But when you have satori, these miracles will be what you are performing at every moment of life. What distinguishes Christianity from Buddhism, in one respect at least and in the deepest way, is in their way of interpreting miracles. With Buddhists, especially with Zen followers, their life is a series of miracles. They do not perform them at a certain specified place and in a certain specified time, as Christ did. It was Jerusalem where he produced a great number of fishes and loaves of bread; it was in Jerusalem and other places that he cast out so many devils. Christians cannot go any further than these deeds of Christ; they cannot transform their whole life into one grand miracle.

When Shomatsu (1799–1871) of Sanuki was warned

against Christianity's overriding Japan, he said: "I am not worried about it. No religion could be better than the one which turns most ordinary sinful souls into Buddhas." Is this not the miraculous event—that we sinful mortals are all transformed just as we are into enlightened ones? Buddhism, especially Zen, claims to execute this miracle by means of satori. The miracle in Buddhist terminology is known as *acintya-moksha*, "unthinkable emancipation".

One may ask: "How could such a miracle be performed by one act of satori? How could we, limited as we are in every possible way, intellectually, physically, morally, and otherwise, ever expect to achieve such a wonder of wonders?"

If satori were a special act to be carried out by a special faculty of mind, like seeing by the eye, or hearing by the ear, it could never manage to comprehend the continuum. The continuum thus comprehended will be an object among many other objects, one of the multitudes, one particularized by means of intellect, and will vanish into the body of the continuum itself. There will still be another continuum left which is to be prehended somehow. As for satori itself, it will turn into an act or a form of intuition. Zen does not propose this kind of miracle. In satori the continuum is not subjected to the process of intellection and differentiation; it is not a concept here, though we have to speak of it as if it were. Satori is the continuum becoming conscious of it. When it perceives itself as it is in itself there is a satori. Therefore there is in satori no differentiation of subject and object. What is perceived is the percipient itself, and the percipient is no other body than the perceived; the two are in a perfect state of identification; even to speak of identification is apt to mislead us to the assumption of two objects which are identified by an act of intuition.

Satori is not, therefore, to be confused with intuition. There have never been two from the very first. It was the human act of knowing that God divided himself and came to be conscious of himself as not God and yet God. Therefore Zen starts with negation, with denying knowledge,

with contradicting human experience which is funda-
mentally conditioned in bifurcation. Zen has realized that
this is the only way to reach the bottomless abyss of the
Godhead where God remains God and no process of
becoming not-God has yet begun. Here we cannot talk
about intuition or identification; there is only an absolute
state of self-identity. Silence is probably the most eloquent
way of indicating or suggesting it. But silence from the
human point of view lends itself most readily to all kinds of
misinterpretation, hence of falsification. It is for this
reason that Zen resorts to such paradoxes as these:

"I am facing you all day long yet we have never met
since eternity."

"I have been in a state of enlightenment even prior to
the appearance of the first Buddha."

"Behold, the whole range of eastern hills is walking on
the waters."

Someone asked the master, "How do we escape this
intense heat of the midsummer day?" Said the master,
"Why not leap into the midst of the boiling water, of the
blazing furnace?" "How could one escape," the monk
was persistent, "from the intensity of this heat?" The
master immediately responded, "The cooling breeze blows
over the quiet sea!"

These Zen expressions are not meant just to contradict our sense-intellect experiences. They are, on the
contrary, the most natural utterances of satori. Or you
can say that these are the Zen way of reaffirming our
experience, not indeed from the partial and therefore
inevitably distorted point of view as engendered by the
intellect, but from the totalistic point of view in which
reality is grasped not only in its atomic and disconnected
aspects but also as the undifferentiated, undetermined
continuum. In conformity with this view gained in satori,
the Zen master is a most ordinary man with no mysteries,
with no miracles about him; he is not distinguishable
from a man in the street. He talks conventionally, acts
like a sensible man, and eats and drinks like ordinary
human beings.

Chokei Ryo (853–932) once produced his staff before
the congregation, saying, "When you understand this,
your discipline in Zen comes to a finish." Is this not plain
and simple enough? Zen is just a matter of a stick. When
you know it, you know the undifferentiated continuum.
There is no mystification about it.

When a monk came to Dogo Chi (779–835) and asked,
"What is the deepest secret you have finally come to?"
Dogo came down from his chair, bowed to the visitor and
said, "You are welcome, indeed, coming from afar, but I
am sorry I have not much to entertain you." Is this not
the most ordinary way of receiving visitors among us?
And is this Dogo's deepest satori which he got before
the light flashed from God's command, "Let there be
light"?

Ryutan Shin stayed with Tenno (748–807) for three
years, but having no instructions in Zen, as he expected,
he asked, "It is some time since my arrival here, but I
have yet had no words from you, master, in the way of
spiritual teaching." Said the Master, "Ever since your
arrival here I have been teaching you in matters of
spiritual enlightenment." Ryutan did not understand this
and asked again, "When were such matters ever imparted
to me?" The master's reply was: "When you bring me tea
to drink, do I not take it? When you bring me food to
eat, do I not accept it? When you bow to me, do I not
acknowledge it by nodding? When was I ever at fault in
instructing you in matters spiritual?" Dogo stood still
for a while thinking about it. The master said, "If you
want to see into the matter, see it at once; deliberation
makes you miss the point for ever." This is said to have
awakened the disciple to the truth of Zen.

A remarkable story indeed. The most innocent and
in a way "irreligious" affairs of our routine life are turned
into matters of deep spiritual significance. God in heaven
is brought down to earth and made to talk with us and
to us in a familiar way. While Zen makes the master's
staff go through a supernatural transformation, and,
turning it into a dragon, makes it swallow up the whole

universe,[1] it settles down on the other hand to most insignificant incidents of life and finds itself comfortably satisfied with them. Here God is found not as an august being inspiring awe and tremulation, but as one intimately familiar and approachable and lovable.

When satori is made to scale heaven and earth and to plunge headlong into the midst of the chaotic undifferentiated continuum, we are apt to take it as something altogether beyond our lackadaisical life. But when we come across such stories as exemplified by Ryutan and Tenno, satori faces us as a thing quite within our hold, something even a plain-thinking peddler might be induced to grapple with.

Haku-un Tan (1025–1072) composed the following verse on Tenno's "spiritual" instruction given to Ryutan:

> Putting aside his layman's white dress,
> He comes to the Zen master and tastes bitter hardships:
> He takes the tea reverentially to the master;
> He looks after his well-being with love and devotion.
> One day, as if incidentally, he reviews
> Affairs of the past three years;
> Would not this evoke the street-vendor's hearty laugh
> Who goes peddling pastry before the temple steps?

II

Satori obtains when eternity cuts into time or impinges upon time, or, which is the same thing after all, when time emerges itself into eternity. Time means *shabetsu*, differentiation and determination, while eternity is *byodo*, all that is not *shabetsu*. Eternity impinging upon time will then mean that *byodo* and *shabetsu* interpenetrate each other, or to use Kegon terminology, the interfusion of *ri*

---

[1] It was Ummon who made his staff turn into a dragon and made the dragon swallow up the entire universe.

(the universal) and *ji* (the individual). But as Zen is not interested so much in conceptualization as in "existential thinking" so-called, satori is said to take place when consciousness realizes a state of "one thought". "One thought", *ichinen* in Japanese and probably *ekakshana* in Sanskrit, is the shortest possible unit of time. Just as English-speaking people say "quick as thought", thought, i.e. *nen*, represents an instant, i.e. time reduced to an absolute point with no durability whatever. The Sanskrit *kshana* means both thought and instant. When time is reduced to a point with no durability, it is "absolute present" or "eternal now". From the point of view of existential thinking, this "absolute present" is no abstraction, no logical nothingness; it is, on the contrary, alive with creative vitality.

Satori is the experience of this fact. Buddhist scholars often define *ichinen*, "one thought", as a point of time which has neither the past nor the future, that is to say, *ichinen* is where eternity cuts into time, and when this momentous event takes place it is known as satori.

It now goes without saying that satori is not stopping the flow of consciousness, as is sometimes erroneously contended. This error comes from taking *samadhi* as preliminary to the experience of satori and then confusing *samadhi* with the suspension of thoughts—a psychological state of utter blankness, which is another word for death. Eternity has a death-aspect, too, as long as it remains in itself, that is, as long as it remains an abstraction like other generalized ideas.

Eternity to be alive must come down into the order of time where it can work out all its possibilities, whereas time left to itself has no field of operation. Time must be merged into eternity, when it gains its meaning. Time by itself is non-existent very much in the way that eternity is impotent without time. It is in our actual living of eternity that the notion of time is possible. Each moment of living marks the steps of eternity. To take hold of eternity, therefore, consciousness must be awakened just at the very moment when eternity lifts its feet to step into time. This moment is what is known as the "absolute present" or "eternal now". It is an absolute point of time where there is no past left behind, no future waiting ahead. Satori stands at this point, where potentialities are about to actualize themselves. Satori does not come out of death; it is at the very moment of actualization. It is in fact the moment itself, which means that it is life as it lives itself.

The bifurcation of reality is the work of the intellect; indeed it is the way in which we try to understand it in order to make use of it in our practical life. But this is not the way to understand reality to the satisfaction of our hearts. The bifurcation helps us to handle reality, to make it work for our physical and intellectual needs, but in truth it never appeals to our inmost needs. For the latter purpose reality must be taken hold of as we immediately experience it. To set it up, for instance, in space and time, murders it. This is the fundamental mistake we have committed in the understanding of reality. At the beginning of the intellectual awakening we thought we achieved a grand feat in arranging reality within the frame of time and space. We never thought this was really preparing for a spiritual tragedy.

Things are made to expand in space and to rise and disappear in time; a world of multitudes is now conceived. Spatially, we are unable to see the furthest limits; temporally, we desire to fix the beginning and end of things, which, however, defy the efforts of our scientists and philosophers. We are thus kept prisoners in the system of our own fabrication. And we are most discontented prisoners, kicking furiously against the fates. We have systematized things by means of space and time, but space and time are terribly disturbing ideas.

Space is not time, time is not space; infinite expansion cannot be made to harmonize with perpetual transformation; the spatial conception of the world tends to keep things stabilized in the Absolute, while its temporal interpretation keeps us in a most uneasy frame of mind. We crave for something eternal and yet we are for ever subjected to states of transience. A life of sixty or seventy years is not at all satisfying, and all the work we can accomplish during these short intervals does not amount to much.

Take nations instead of individuals; their time-allowance may be longer, but what difference do they make in cycles of millenniums? Cultures are more enduring and seem to have some worth. But if we are encompassed in vastness of space and endlessness of time, what are they with all the philosophers, artists, and with all the generals and strategists? Are they not all like vanishing foam or shooting stars?

Men of satori are not, however, worried about these things. For satori stands firmly on the Absolute Present, Eternal Now, where time and space are coalesced and yet begin to get differentiated. They lie there dormant, as it were, with all their futurities and possibilities; they are both there rolled up with all their achievements and unfoldments. It is the privilege of satori, sitting in the Absolute Present, quietly to survey the past and contemplate the future. How does the Zen master enjoy this privilege, we may ask? The following sermon given by Ummon is illustrative of this point. (Ummon of the tenth century is the founder of the school bearing his name, and one of the most astute exponents of Zen.) His sermon runs thus:

"I am not going to ask you anything about what has preceded this day, the fifteenth of the month, but let me have a word about what is to follow this day, the fifteenth."

So saying he gave his "word": "Every day a fine day."

A few words of comment are needed. As we know, the original Chinese is very vague. Literally, it reads, "The fifteenth day before, I do not ask; the fifteenth day after, bring me a word (or a sentence)." But what is the subject about which Ummon requests "no asking"? What is again the subject regarding which he wants to have "a word"? Nothing is specified. But in fact no such specifications are needed here. What Ummon wants is to make us grasp the absolute "fifteenth day of the month". The absolute fifteenth is the Absolute Present completely cut off from the past fifteen days as well as from the coming fifteen days. One who has truly grasped the "fifteenth" can give the "word" which Ummon requests.

Ummon's own was, "Every day is a fine day" (literally, "Day after) day, this (a) fine day"). This singularly corresponds to Eckhart's beggar's greeting, "Every morning is a good morning," which was given in answer to a conventional "Good morning." Ummon's statement in itself seems simple and ordinary, and we may not at once see when and how this is connected with the absolute "fifteenth".

To trace this connection a rather rationalistic explanation may be needed. Ummon's sermon or request is superficially innocent enough, but really it is a terrific challenge to our rationalistic way of thinking. Zen abhors this, and desires not to have anything to do with logic and abstraction. But, humanly speaking, we cannot very well escape it. With all the limitations of human consciousness, we do our utmost to express the inexpressible.

Ever since *avidya* (Ignorance) asserted itself we take great pleasure in dividing up reality into pieces; we divide time into years, months, days, hours, seconds, and this second into millions of infinitesimal parts. But, for all practical purposes, a year of twelve months and a month of thirty days works quite well. Ummon and his disciples found themselves standing on the line of time-division, the day being the fifteenth of the month. The line does not belong to the preceding fifteen days, nor can it be classed with the fifteen days to come. The past is past, and the future is not yet here. The line is the absolute line of the Present, altogether timeless, as a spatial, geometrical line has no width. But, existentially speaking, the absolute "fifteenth day" is not empty and contentless; in it indeed are hoarded up all the past deeds or achievements already taking effect, and also all the possibilities that are to materialize in time to come.

How would the Zen master give expression to this

fact? He is not a dialectician, not a metaphysician, he is not used to subtleties of intellection. He is a most practical man, in the sense of a radical empiricist; he does not conceptualize. Hence Ummon's utterance, "Every day is a fine day." This is his description of the Absolute Present seen from his viewpoint of satori. And it is well to remember that this kind of description, directly issuing out of experience and not elaborated by the intellect, is permitted only to men of satori.

As far as satori itself is concerned, a reference to the past fifteen days of the month and also to another fifteen days to come is irrelevant. The reference here, however, supplies a background to Ummon's direct statement; it makes the latter stand out more intelligibly; it is, further, a kind of decoy whereby to catch the real thing. For this reason Ummon's statement in regard to the fifteenth day of the month need not be made the special object of attention. The idea is to get the audience's mind centred in the "Absolute Present", not conditioned by the future as well as the past. This is the day dividing the month into two, with the fifteen days ahead and the fifteen days behind; if so, it cannot be called one of the past fifteen days, nor is it proper to take it for one of the coming fifteen days. What is past is no more here, and what is to come is not yet here; could Ummon's "fifteenth day" be merely chimerical? But he, including all his disciples, are decidedly living the fifteenth of the month as determined by the calendar of that day.

"A word" must be given to this real "existence", however dialectically it is non-existent. Engo of the Sung dynasty, who commented on Ummon in his *Hekigan-Shu*, says in essence: "When he refers to the past fifteen days and to the fifteen days to follow, he is not restrained by a world of differentiation; he overrides all the ten thousand things of determination. If we are retained by words and try to interpret him accordingly, we shall be farthest away from him." Ummon is not to be reached by means of mere concepts and their manipulation.

Setcho (980–1052), a great literary genius and one of

the foremost Zen masters of the Sung Dynasty belonging
to Ummon's school, composed a poem on "The Fifteenth
Day" of his predecessor:

> Put one aside,
> Hold on to seven.
> Heaven above and earth below and the four quarters,
> Nowhere his equal is to be found. (1)
> He walks quietly on the murmuring waters of the
>   stream;
> He surveys the sky and traces the shadow of the flying
>   bird. (2)
> The weeds grow rampant,
> The clouds are densely overhanging. (3)
> Around the cave the flowers are showered where
>   Subhuti is lost in meditation;
> The advocate of the Void deserves pity as much as
>   contempt. (4)
> No wavering here!
> If you do, thirty blows! (5)

Setcho's verse is cryptic, and may require notes to
make the sense accessible to the ordinary reader:

(1) The numerals one and seven here have not much
to do with the main theme except to remind us of Ummon's
"fifteen" or "fifteenth". "To put one aside" and "to hold
on to seven", therefore, convey no real meaning, they just
purport to give a warning against attaching oneself to
numbers, that is concepts, and getting hopelessly entangled
in dialectical meshes. When, however, one is freed from
such attachments and entanglements, one is "the only
honoured one in heaven above and on earth below"—the
utterance legendarily ascribed to Buddha at his birth.

(2) When "the only honoured one" makes his appearance, he works miracles all round. He walks quietly on
the stream and its waters safely sustain him; he gazes at
airy nothing and can chalk out the traces left by the
flying bird.

These are, however, only symbolic of the far greater
and essentially characteristic miracle which he performs,

for though he may live in a most prosaic and karma-bound way, yet in his inner life he is not at all bound by karma, or fettered by laws; he is free, and the master of himself in every sense of the word. He has grasped the Absolute Present, he lives in it, though apparently his life is regulated like ours in time and by its limitations. He is dead in Adam (time and space) and lives in Christ (Absolute Present). He may be in the midst of a blazing fire, and is not hurt; he may be swallowed up by the waves of the ocean, and is not drowned. Why? Because he is now Life itself—Life out of which time and space are woven.

(3) While satori has its own world, it is also discoverable in a world of multitudes. Indeed, if it avoids the latter, it cannot be a genuine satori. It ought never to be identified with Emptiness (*sunyata*), inert and contentless. Hence the weeds are growing luxuriantly, and clouds hang heavily. Satori is to thrive in differentiation. As it transcends time and space and their determinations, it is also in them. When thoroughly immersed in them and identified with them, satori becomes meaningful.

(4) The gods and all other heavenly beings may have an unmixed feeling of reverence for the One who has detached himself from all worldly ties and passions and is living in the Void; they may shower heavenly flowers over Subhuti, the ascetic, completely absorbed in a self-denying and world-forgetting *samadhi* (meditation), but satori is not there. On the contrary, it looks down with pity, if not with disdain, on such onesided transcendentalism or all-annihilating absolutism.

(5) On this point we are not allowed to waver; no compromise is possible; the way of satori lies ahead of us clear of all dualistic complexities. If we cannot go straight forward with satori in the Absolute Present, we shall certainly deserve Setcho's thirty blows.

III

The following story will help to make us acquainted with the Zen master's way of leading his disciples to the lively content of the Absolute Present.

Baso (–788) had a walk one day with Hyakujo (–814), one of his pupils. Seeing a flock of wild geese flying across the sky, he said, "What are they?" Answered Hyakujo, "They are wild geese, master." Baso asked again, "Whither are they flying?" "They are all gone now." Baso turned towards Hyakujo and gave a twist to his nose. Feeling much pain Hyakujo gave a suppressed cry. Baso immediately pursued, "Are they really gone?"

This awakened Hyakujo to a state of satori, and the experience was demonstrated on the following day when the master mounted the platform to give his congregation a talk on Zen. Hyakujo came forward and began to roll up the matting which is generally spread before the master for his disciples to make their bows to him. This rolling up as a rule means the end of the session. Baso came down from his seat and left for his room.

Hyakujo was called in, and Baso said, "When I have not said a word why did you roll up the matting?"

Hyakujo said, "Yesterday you were kind enough to give my nose a twist which pained me very much."

"Where is your mind wandering today?"

"The nose does not hurt me any more today."

"You have indeed a deep insight into the matter of 'this day'," was Baso's testimony.

"This Day" here means the Absolute Present and corresponds to Ummon's "The Fifteenth Day". "This day" of "today" is *konnichi* in Japanese, for which a more expressive term is often used by the Zen masters, that is, *sokkon*. *Soku* is a difficult term to translate; it means "just this", or abstractly, "self-identity"; *sokkon*, therefore, is "this very moment" and the master would often demand, "What is the matter of this very moment?"

When Baso twisted Hyakujo's nose his idea was to make his disciple awake to the fact of the Absolute

Present, and not to be just concerned with flying birds. The birds are in space and fly in time; you look at them and you put yourself immediately in space-relations; you observe that they are flying, and this at once confines you in the frame of time. As soon as you are in the system of time and space, you step off the Absolute Présent, which means that you are no more a free, self-regulating spirit, but a mere man, karma-fettered and logically-minded. Satori never comes out of such existence. Hence Baso's boundless love which prompted him to give a twist to Hyakujo's nose. The pain itself had nothing to do with Hyakujo's satori itself. The incident afforded him an opportunity to break up the framework of consciousness, which vigorously and tyrannically places the mind under the rules of space and time and consequently of logical conceptualization.

The master's business is to take away these shackles from the disciple's mind. He does this generally by means of negations or contradictions, proposing "to see a rainfall suspended", or "not to call a fan a fan, or a spade a spade". This may still have a trace of intellection, but the twisting of the nose, or the kicking at the chest, or the shaking by the collar is something utterly unheard of in the annals of spiritual discipline. But its effectiveness has repeatedly and fully been proved by the Zen masters.

It is interesting to cite the sequence of the Hyakujo incident, for it was quite dramatic. When he returned to his own quarters from his interview with Baso in regard to the rolling-up of the matting he was found to be crying aloud. A brother-monk anxiously inquired what was the matter with him. But Hyakujo said, "You go to the master and find out for yourself what is the matter with me."

The brother-monk went to Baso and asked about Hyakujo. Baso said, "You go back to him and find it out directly from him." The brother-monk came back to Hyakujo and asked him about it again. But Hyakujo, instead of answering him, burst into a roar of laughter. The monk was nonplussed. "A while ago you were crying, and how is it that you are laughing now?" Hyakujo was nonchalant and said, "I was crying before, but I am now laughing."

Undoubtedly, Hyakujo must have undergone a deep psychological change since his nose was pinched by his master Baso. He evidently realized that there was another life than that which is under the enthralment of the time-concept, that is, generally found ruminating over the frustrations of the past and looking forward, full of anguish, to events yet to happen.

The Hyakujo now crying, now laughing, does not lose sight of the Absolute Present. Before his satori his crying or laughing was not a pure act. It was always mixed with something else. His unconscious consciousness of time urged him to look forward, if not thinking of the past. As the result, he was vexed with a feeling of tension, which is unnecessarily exhausting. His mind was never complete in itself; it was divided, torn to pieces, and could not be "one whole mind" (*isshin* or *ichinen*). It lost its resting-place, balance, stillness. Most modern minds are, therefore, neurotics, victims of logical confusion and psychological tension.

IV

In "Our Sense of the Present", an article in the *Hibbert Journal*, April number, 1946, the author, Ethel M. Rowell, refers to "a stillness which abides in the present, and which we can experience here and now". This stillness, this timeless time, is "the instant made eternity", that is, it is the moment infinitely expanding—"one moment, one and infinite". The writer's characterization of the sense of the Present is very informing in its connection with satori as explained in this chapter. But she does not go very far beyond describing the sense itself. "Ultimately a sense of the Present is perhaps a reflection in us of the presence of Him who is always present, who himself is the eternity at the heart of the present, 'the still point of the turning world'. And to learn to rest in the present is perhaps a first step towards the 'practice of the presence of God'."

This is tentative enough, but does not open up to a satori. The mere feeling for the present is not enough to make one leap into the eternity and self-sufficiency of the Present.

The feeling still leaves something dualistic, whereas satori is the Absolute Present itself. And because of this, the experience goes along with every other experience growing out of the serialistic conception of time. Hence Hyakujo's remarks: "It pained me yesterday but it does not today," "I am laughing now though I was crying a little while ago." Out of such daily experience as pain and no-pain, crying and laughing, human consciousness weaves a time-continuum, and regards it as reality.

When this is accomplished, the procedure is now reversed, and we begin to build up our experiences on the screen of time. Serialism comes first now, and we find our lives miserably bound by it. The Absolute Present is pushed back; we are no more conscious of it. We regret the past and worry about the future. Our crying is not pure crying, nor is our laughing pure laughing. There is always something else mixed up with it; that is, the present has lost its innocence and absoluteness. The future and the past overlay the present and suffocate it. Life is now a suffocated one, maimed and crippled.

A Vinaya[1] teacher once asked a Zen master:

"How do you discipline yourself in your daily life?"

The master said: "When I am hungry I eat, when I feel tired I sleep."

Teacher: "That is what everybody does. Could they be said to be disciplining themselves as much as yourself?"

Master: "No, not in the same way."

[1] *Vinaya* in Sanskrit means "rules of moral discipline", forming one of the three departments of the Buddhist teaching. Sutras, which are Buddha's personal discourses, Vinaya, rules laid down by Buddha for his disciples of various grades; and Abhidharma, philosophical treatises dealing with Buddhist thought.

Teacher: "Why not the same?"

Master: "When they eat, they dare not eat, their minds are filled with all kinds of contrivances. Therefore, I say, not the same."

E. M. Rowell cites in her article the story of a London woman after an air raid during the war: "After a night of blitz a woman was seen to come repeatedly to the door of her battered little house and to look anxiously up and down the street. An official approached her. "Can I do anything to help you?" She answered, "Well, have you seen the milkman anywhere about? My man always likes his early cup of tea." And the author adds: "The past was hostile, the future unreliable, but the companionable present was there with her. Life was precarious, but —her husband wanted his early cup of tea!"

The only difference between the Zen master who ate and slept heartily and the London woman who wanted milk for her husband's early cup of tea is that the one had satori while the other was just an ordinary human; the one deeply looked into the secrets of the Absolute Present which is also "this present little instant" of everybody and of the whole world, while most of us, including the other, are experiencing it and have a feeling for it, but have not yet had any satori about it.

We read in the Bible (Matt. vi, 34) : "Take therefore no thought for the morrow; for the morrow shall take thought for the things of itself. Sufficient unto the day is the evil thereof." The idea expressed here by Jesus exactly corresponds to the Zen conception of the Absolute Present. Zen has its own way of presenting the idea, and its satori may seem remote from the Christian feeling. But when Christians stand all naked, shorn of their dualistic garments, they will discover that their God is no other than the Absolute Present itself.

They generally think of him as putting on so many ethical and spiritual appendages, which in fact keep him away from them; they somehow hesitate to appear before him in their nakedness, that is, to take hold of him in the Absolute Present. The Christian sense of the Absolute

Present does not come to a focus and crystallize, as it were, into a satori; it is too diffused, or still contains a residue of time-serialism.

Zen has several names for satori as it is observed in its relationship with various fields of human experience. Some of them are "the mind that has no abode", "the mind that owns nothing", "the homeless mind", "the unattached mind", "mindlessness", "thoughtlessness", "the one mind". These designations all refer to the popular conception of "mind", and Zen strongly denies its existence as reality. But this denial is not the outcome of rationalization, being based on actual experience. The dualistic notion of mind or thought and matter has been the bane of human consciousness, and we have been prevented from properly understanding ourselves. For this reason, Zen is most emphatic in its insistence on "mindlessness", and this not proved syllogistically but as a matter of fact.

To clear consciousness of any trace of attachment to the mind-concept, Zen proposes various practical methods, one of which is, according to Daishyu Yekai, a disciple of Baso, as follows:[1]

"If you wish to have a clear insight into the mind that has no abode, you have it at the very moment when you are sitting (in the right mood of meditation). Then you see that the mind is altogether devoid of thoughts, that it is not thinking of ideas, good or evil.

"Things past are already past, and when you do not pursue them, the past mind disappears by itself, together with its contents. As to things that are to come, have no hankerings after them, do not have them conjured up in imagination. Then the future mind will disappear by itself with all its possible contents. Things that are at this moment before your mind are already here. What is important in regard to things generally is not to get attached to them. When the mind is not attached, it raises no thoughts of love or hate, and the present mind will disappear by itself with all its contents.

[1] From *Essentials of the Abrupt Understanding*, by *Daishu Yekai*.

"When your mind is thus not contained in the three divisions of time (past, future, and present), it can be said that the mind is not in time (i.e. it is a state of timelessness).

"If the mind should be stirred up, do not follow the stirrings, and the following-up mind will by itself disappear. When the mind abides with itself, do not hold on to this abiding, and the abiding mind will by itself disappear. Thus when the no-abiding mind obtains, this is abiding in no-abode.

"When you have a clear cognizance of this state of mind, your abiding mind is just abiding and yet not abiding at all in any particular abode. When it is not abiding it is not conscious of any particular abode to be known as no-abiding. When you have thus a clear insight into the state of consciousness not abiding anywhere (that is, when it is not fixed at any particular object of thought), you are said to have a clear insight into the original mind. This is also known as seeing into one's own being. The mind that has no abode anywhere is no other than the Buddha-mind."

This no-abiding mind is the Absolute Present, for it has no abode anywhere in the past, or in the future or in the present; the mind is not what it is commonly understood to be by those not yet awakened by satori.

Daishu says somewhere else in his book on *Abrupt Awakening* that "when the mind penetrates through This Instant, what is before and what is after are manifested at once to this mind; it is like the past Buddhas at once facing the future Buddhas; the ten-thousand things (concur) simultaneously. Where all things are known in one thought, this is the spiritual field, for all-knowledge is attained here." All these things are possible only when one's mind is awakened to the Absolute Present, not as a logical conclusion, but as satori consciousness.

An old woman kept a tea-house at the foot of the Ryutan monastery in Reishu. Tokusan (780–865), who later became noted for his staff, dropped in at the tea-house by the roadside while on pilgrimage in search of a good Zen master. He was a scholar of the Vajracchedika Sutra (*Diamond Sutra*), but hearing of Zen, which taught that the mind itself was Buddha, he could not accept it and wanted to interview a Zen student. Shouldering his precious commentary on the Sutra, he left his abode in Szu-chuan.

He asked the old woman to serve him a *ten-jin*. *Ten-jin* means refreshments, but literally "mind-dotting". She asked what was in his rucksack. He said, "This is a commentary on the *Diamond Sutra*."

The old woman resumed: "I have a question to ask you. If your answer is satisfactory I will serve you refreshments free. If otherwise, you will have to go somewhere else."

Tokusan said, "Well, I am ready."

The question was this: "According to the *Diamond Sutra*, we have, 'The past mind is unattainable, the present mind is unattainable, the future mind is unattainable.' Now, which mind is it you want to dot?"

This baffled the *Diamond* scholar, and the old woman let him go somewhere else for his refreshments.

I do not know how *ten-jin*, literally "mind-dotting", came to mean refreshments, but the old woman made a very pungent use of the character, *jin* or *shin* (mind), to put the proud scholar's mind at the impasse. Whatever this be, how should we understand the statement in the *Diamond Sutra*? What does the mind past, present, and future mean? What is the signification of "unattainable"?

When satori obtains in the Absolute Present, all these questions solve themselves. The mind or consciousness, serially divided and developed in time, always escapes our prehension, is never "attainable" as to its reality. It is only when our unconscious consciousness, or what might be called super-consciousness, comes to itself, is awakened to itself, that our eyes open to the timelessness of the present in which and from which divisible time unfolds itself and reveals its true nature.

Tokusan, still uninitiated in the mystery of satori at

the time of his interview with the old lady of the tea-house, could not understand what her question purported. His conception of time was gained from his pet commentary by Seiryo, which meant that his understanding could not go beyond logical reasonableness; the distance between this and satori was immeasurable, for the difference was not one of calculability, but of order, of quality, of value. The gap between satori and rationality could never be bridged by concept-making and postulation, but by an absolute negation of the reason itself, which means "an existential leap".

V

Another name for satori is *kensho*, "seeing into one's own nature". This may suggest the idea that there is what is known as nature or substance making up one's being, and that this nature is seen by somebody standing against it. That is to say, there is one who sees and there is another which is seen, subject and object, master and guest. This view is the one generally held by most of us, for our world is a rational reconstruction which keeps one thing always opposing another, and by means of this opposition we think, and our thinking in turn is projected into every field of experience; hence this dichotomous world multiplying itself infinitely.

Kensho, on the contrary, means going against this way of thinking and putting an end to all forms of dualism. This really means reconstructing our experience from its very foundation. What Zen attempts is no other than the most radical revolution of our world-view.

The rationalistic way of dissolving contradictory concepts is to create a third concept in which they can be harmoniously set up. To find out such a new concept is the work taken up by the philosopher. While it is a great question whether he can finally succeed in discovering an all-embracing and all-uniting and all-harmonizing concept, we cannot stop short of arriving at such a result as far as our intellect is concerned. Endless and fruitless may be our efforts, but we shall have to go on this way.

The Zen way has taken an altogether different course, diametrically opposed to the logical or philosophical method. It is not that Zen is defiantly antagonistic to the latter, for Zen is also ready to recognize the practical usefulness of the intellect and willing to give it the proper place it deserves. But Zen has advocated another method of reaching the finality of things, where the spirit lies at rest with itself as well as with the world at large. It tells us to retreat to our inner self in which no bifurcation has yet taken place. Ordinarily, we go out of ourselves to seek a place of ultimate rest. We walk on and on until we reach God, who is at the head of a long tedious series of bifurcations and unifications.

Zen takes the opposite course and steps backwards, as it were, to reach the undifferentiated continuum itself. It looks backwards to a point before the world with all its dichotomies has yet made its début. This means that Zen wants us to face a world into which time and space have not yet put their cleaving wedges. What kind of experience is this? Our experience has always been conditioned by logic, by time, and by space. Experience will be utterly impossible if it is not so conditioned. To refer to experience free from such conditions is nonsensical, one may say. Perhaps it is, so long as we uphold time and space as real and not conceptually projected. But even when these basic conditions of experience are denied, Zen talks of a certain kind of experience. If this be really the case, Zen experience must be said to take place in the timelessness of the Absolute Present.

Do not ask how this is possible, for its possibility has been all the time demonstrated by Zen. We must remember that the realm of Zen is where no rationality holds good; in fact it supplies the field of operation for it; we can say that with the Zen experience all the rationalistic superstructure finds its solid basis.

Incidentally we may remark that the Christian view of the world starts with "the tree of knowledge", whereas the Buddhist world is the outcome of Ignorance (*avidya*). Buddhists, therefore, negate the world as the thing most needed for reaching the final abode of rest. Ignorance is conquered only when the state of things prior to Ignorance is realized, which is satori, seeing into one's own nature as it is by itself, not obscured by Ignorance. Ignorance is the beginning of knowledge, and the truth of things is not to be attained by piling knowledge upon knowledge, which means no more, no less, than intensifying Ignorance.

From this Buddhist point of view Christians are all the time rushing into Ignorance when they think they are increasing the amount of knowledge by logical acumen and analytical subtlety. Buddhists want us to see our own "original face" even before we were born, to hear the cry of the crow even before it was uttered, to be with God even before he commanded light to be. Christians take God and his light as things irrevocable, imperatively imposed upon them, and start their work of salvation under these limitations. Their "knowledge" always clings to them, they cannot shake this shackle off; they become victims of logic and rationality. Logic and rationality are all very well, Buddhists say, but the real spiritual abode, according to Buddhists, is found only where logic and rationality have not yet made their start, where there is yet no subject to assert itself, no object to be taken hold of; where there is neither seer nor the seen, which is "seeing into one's own nature".

VI

Satori, or the "seeing into one's own nature", is frequently confused with nothingness or emptiness, which is a pure state of negativity. Superficially, this seems to be justifiable. For, logically speaking, the mind awakened to the timelessness of time has no content, does not convey any sense of actual experience. As to "seeing into one's own nature", if this means a state of consciousness where there is neither the seeing subject nor the object seen, it cannot be anything else but a state of pure emptiness, which has no significance whatever for our everyday life, which is full of frustrations and expectations and vexations. This is true as far as our dualistic thinking is concerned. But we must remember that Zen deals with the most fundamental and most concrete experience lying at the basis of our daily living. Being an individual experience and not the conclusion of logical reasoning, it is neither abstract nor empty. On the contrary, it is most concrete, and filled with possibilities.

If satori were a mere empty abstraction or generalization it could not be the basis of the ten thousand things. Rationalization goes upwards, getting rid of multiplicities step by step, and finally reaches a point which has no width, no breadth, merely indicating a position. But satori digs downwards under the ground of all existence in order to reach the rock which is an undifferentiated whole. It is not something floating in the air, but a solid substantial entity, though not in the sense of an individual sense-object.

In conformity with the common-sense way of thinking, Zen frequently uses terms which are liable to be misunderstood. Thus the term "nature" affords good opportunity for misinterpretation. We are apt to take it for something underlying a phenomenal sense-object, thought existing in a much more subtle way, but satori does not consist in seeing such subtle object; for in the satori seeing there is neither subject nor object; it is at once seeing and not seeing; that which is seen is that which sees, and *vice versa*. As subject and object are thus one in the satori seeing, it is evident that it is not seeing in the ordinary dualistic sense. And this has led many superficially-minded people to imagine that Zen's seeing is seeing into the Void, being absorbed in contemplation, and not productive of anything useful for our practical life.

The great discovery we owe Buddhism, and especially Zen, is that it has opened for us the way to see into the suchness of things, which is to have an insight into "the originally pure in essence and form which is the ocean of transcendental Prajna-knowledge", as Gensha says in one of his sermons. "The originally pure" is "a stillness which abides in the present".

Buddhists use the word "pure" in the sense of absolute, and not in that of freedom from dirt and external matters. "The originally pure" means that which is unconditioned, undifferentiated, and devoid of all determinations; it is a kind of super-consciousness in which there is no opposition of subject and object, and yet there is a full awareness of things that are to follow as well as things already fulfilled. In a sense "the originally pure" is emptiness, but an emptiness charged with vitality. Suchness is, therefore, the two contradictory concepts, emptiness and not-emptiness, in a state of self-identity. Suchness is not their synthesis but their self-identity as concretely realized in our everyday experience.

What we have to remember here is that the concept of suchness is not the result of rationalistic thinking about experience but just a plain direct description of it. When we see a white flower we describe it as white; when it is a red one, we say it is red. This is simply a factual statement of the senses; we have not reasoned about redness or whiteness, we just see things red or white, and declare them so. In a similar way, Zen sees with its satori-eye things as they are in themselves, i.e. they are seen as such—such as they are, no more, no less, and Zen says so.

We as human beings, Zen proclaims, cannot go any further than this. Science and philosophy will say that our senses are not reliable; nor is the intellect; they are not to be depended upon as the absolutely trustworthy instrument of knowledge, and, therefore, that the Zen view of suchness cannot be regarded either as the last source of authority. This analogy, however, does not hold good in the case of Zen, because the satori-seeing cannot be classed under the same category as the sense-information. In satori there is something more, though this something is something absolutely unique and can be appreciated only by those who have had its experience.

This, it is true, is the case with all feelings, the feeling

that you are an absolutely unique individuality, the feeling that the life you are enjoying now absolutely belongs
to you, or the feeling that God is giving this special favour
to you alone and to nobody else. But all these feelings
ultimately refer to one definite subject known as "I"
which is differentiated from the rest of the world. Satori is
not a feeling, nor is it an intellectual act generally designated as intuition. Satori is seeing into one's own nature;
and this "nature" is not an entity belonging to oneself as
distinguished from others; and in the "seeing" there is no
seer, there is nothing seen; "Nature" is the seer as well as
the object seen. Satori is "mindlessness", "one absolute
thought", "the absolute present", "originally pure",
"emptiness", "suchness", and many other things.

According to the Zen master, our sense-experience
alone is not enough; nor is intellection, if we wish to
sound the bottomless abyss of reality; satori must be
added to it, not mechanically or quantitatively, but
chemically, as it were, or qualitatively. When we hear a
bell or see a bird flying, we must do so by means of a
mind christened by satori, that is to say, we then hear the
bell even prior to its ringing, and see the bird even prior to
its birth. Once the bell rings or the bird flies, they are
already in the world of the senses, which means that they
are differentiated, subject to intellectual analysis and
synthesis, which means in turn that "the originally pure"
has been adulterated, leading to further and further
adulterations, that there is no longer "the full moon of
suchness" as seen by Buddhist poets, but one now thickly
veiled with threatening clouds. Suchness is synonymous
with pureness.

Gensha (834–908), who flourished towards the close
of the T'ang dynasty, once gave a sermon to the following
effect:

"O monks, have you ever had an insight into the
Originally Pure in essence and form, which is the ocean of
transcendental Prajna-knowledge, or not? If you have had
no insight yet, let me ask you this: You are now gathered
here and do you see the green hills facing us all? If you

say you see them, how do you see them? If you say you do
not, how can you say that, when the hills are confronting
you right here? Do you understand? O monks, it is your
Originally Pure in essence and form which is the ocean of
transcendental Prajna-knowledge that sees and hears to
the fullest extent of its capacity. If you understand, things
are such as they are; if you do not understand, things are
just as they are. . . ."

Gensha, on another occasion, once came into the
Dharma Hall and, hearing the swallows twittering, said,
"They are deeply discoursing on the reality of things; they
are indeed talking well on the essence of the Dharma." So
saying, he descended from the platform. A monk later
accosted him. "Today you were good enough to give us a
sermon on the twittering swallows, but we are unable to
see its meaning." The abbot said, "Did you understand?"
"No, we did not," answered the monk. "Who would ever
believe you?" This was the abbot's verdict.

What does this mondo purport? Gensha and his
disciples could not but hear the swallows twitter, but the
one heard them as discoursing on the deep things of life
while the others did not. Gensha's expression, however, is
conceptual, and we might take him as not being in the
midst of his satori but descending to the level of the
intellect. This is a condescension on the part of Gensha,
whereby he is practising the old woman's Zen, as Zen
people say.

The following one is better.

Gensha once pointed to the lantern and said, "I call
this a lantern, what would you call it?" The disciple
replied, "I too call it a lantern, master." Thereupon
Gensha declared, "Throughout this great Empire
of the T'ang there is not a person who understands
Buddhism."

On another occasion Gensha was not so critical or so
downright outspoken. When he called on Santo, Santo
said, "Living long as I do in a mountain retreat far away
from people, I have no cushion to offer you." Said Gensha,
"Every one of us is supplied with one, and how is it that

you are not provided with one yourself?" Santo now saluted Gensha, saying, "Please take your seat." Gensha said, "Nothing has been lacking from the start."

The following incident recorded of Gensha's activities as a Zen master has something dramatic about it. When his teacher Seppo (822–908) passed away, Gensha, being his foremost disciple, became the chief mourner. The whole congregation assembled, and the tea-offering ceremony was to take place. Gensha in front of his departed teacher's spiritual tablet lifted the tea-cup and asked the congregation: "While our master was still among us, you were free to say whatever you liked. Now that he is no longer here, what would you say? If you can utter a word[1] (suitable for this occasion, on the death of our master), we will consider him faultless; but if you cannot, the fault must be with him. Is there anyone who can utter a word?"

He repeated this three times, but no one was forthcoming. Thereupon Gensha threw the tea-cup down on the floor, breaking it to pieces, and returned to his quarters.

Back in his room, Gensha now asked Chyuto, "How do you understand?" Chyuto said, "What fault did our departed master commit?" Gensha did not say anything, but turned about and sat against the wall (in the meditation posture). Chyuto began to walk away, when Gensha called him back and said to him, "How do you understand?" It was now Chyuto who turned about and sat against the wall. Gensha, satisfied, did not say anything further.

Death is no trivial incident in human affairs, and the ritual in connection with it is naturally coloured with sorrow and deep reflection. Gensha did not forget it, and wished to make good use of the occasion for the edification of his congregation. He wanted the latter to air whatever understanding they had concerning the subject of death.

[1] "To utter a word", or simply, "to say (something)", is Zen's technical way of expressing a view, either in words or in action, proper to the occasion.

He wanted to see how well they had been applying themselves to the mastering of Zen under the guidance of his master, Seppo. Evidently Chyuto was the only person who could "say a word" in regard to the passing of their great master, Seppo. The way they, Chyuto and Gensha, demonstrated Zen between themselves was certainly unique, and proved to be altogether satisfactory to each other, however strange and unapproachable it might appear to outsiders.

Let me remind you here of the fact that they were not committing themselves to this logically unaccountable behaviour just for the sake of appearing so. We must believe that there is such a thing as satori, and that when it is attained we shall understand all the words and deeds recorded of the Zen masters in the history of Zen, which has lasted now for over twelve centuries. Zen is still exercising its spiritually beneficial influence among peoples of the East.

Satori, being beyond the limits of reasonable demonstration, has no fixed, predetermined, authorized methods of proving itself to the uninitiated. The questioners are induced by every possible means to confront it one day in an abrupt manner. As satori has no tangible body to lay hands on, aspirants for it have to evolve it somehow from within themselves. As long as they endeavour to catch a glimpse of it merely from words or acts of the master, it can never be attained. The masters of Zen remain silent in the pulpit and come down without uttering a word. But sometimes they give the shortest possible sermons. Inasmuch as we are endowed with the body, with the tongue, with the hands, all of which are meant to be organs of intelligence and communication, we must be able to make use of them; under proper management they are indeed eloquent and understandable.

Gensha mounted the platform and after a moment of silence gave this out: "Do you know it? Do you now recognize it?" So saying, he went back to his room. Another time, after a silence, he simply said, "This is your true man, just this." Still another time his silence was followed by this: "Daruma[1] is present right here, right now. Do you see him, O monks?"

One day Gensha remained too long in silence, and the monks, thinking he was not going to say anything began, to disperse, when the master called them back and denounced them in the following way: "As I see, you are all cut out of the same pattern; there is none among you who is endowed with any amount of wisdom. When I part my lips you all gather about me wanting to catch my words and speculate on them. But when I really try to do you good, you do not know me. If you go on like this, great trouble is indeed ahead of you."

On another occasion he was a little better, for he gave this after a period of silence, "I am doing what I can for your edification, but do you understand?"

A monk said, "What does it mean when the master, absorbed in silence, utters not a word?"

The master said, "What is the use of talking in sleep?"

The monk continued, "I wish you would enlighten me on matters of fundamental essence."

"What can I do with a sleepy one like you?"

"If I am sleepy, what about you, master?"

"How could you ever be so senseless as not to know where your pain is?" said Gensha.

Sometimes he would say: "Such a big fellow like yourself, how could you wander one thousand or even ten thousand miles, and on reaching here still keep on with your drowsing and drowsy talk? It would be much better just to lie down."

Another monk said, "O master, please be good enough to let me have one word of yours pointing to the essence of the matter."

"When you know it, you have it."

"Please be more direct, O master."

"No use being deaf!" replied the master.

[1] He is the founder of Zen in China. But he is frequently symbolically made use of and stands for Buddha, Buddha-nature, the Absolute, etc. In Gensha's sermon here, Daruma (i.e. Bodhi-Dharma) is quite alive and no abstraction whatever.

When the disciples are earnestly seeking for truth and reality, to call them deaf and sleepy-minded seems to be rather harsh on them. Are the Zen masters such an unkind set of people? Superficially, they are hard-hearted indeed. But to those who know what is what about Zen they are most kindly-disposed. For their remarks come straight from their satori, which is in all sincerity seeking its response in the heart of the disciples.

VII

Seppo, teacher of Gensha, was one of the great masters towards the end of the T'ang dynasty; his *Sayings* are still accessible. One of his favourite answers was, "What is it?" If one should ask him, "What are we facing this very moment?" he would say, "What is it?"

This counter-question on the part of Seppo shows how intimately he feels the presence of "it" or "this". He is desirous to make his questioner apprehend it as intimately as himself, and he does not know how to communicate it without appealing to conceptualism; so he blurts out: "What is this? Cannot you see it? It is right here this very moment. If I resort to words, it is three thousand miles away." "What is this?" is his impatient exclamation. So he says, "Whenever I see my brother monks come, I say, 'What is this?' and they at once try to be long-tongued. As long as they go on like this they will not be able to nod their heads until the year of the ass."[1] All Zen masters hate *talking about* "it", for talking means appealing to intellectualization, which will never bring us to the abode of rest.

The Master An, the national leader of Fu-chou province, saw Seppo first in his Zen career. When Seppo noticed An coming by the gate, he firmly took hold of the newcomer, and said, "What is this?" An was all of a sudden awakened to the signification of it, and raising his

[1] There is no "year of the ass" in the calendar formerly in use in China and Japan. "Until the year of the ass" therefore means "until doomsday".

hands high he danced around. Seppo said, "Do you find anything reasonable about it?" An responded at once. "What reasonableness, master?" Seppo patted him and confirmed his understanding.

Zen masters wish us to see into that unconscious consciousness which accompanies our ordinary dualistically-determined consciousness. The "unconscious" so-called here is not the psychological unconscious, which is regarded as making up the lowest stratum of our mind, probably accumulated ever since we began to become conscious of our own existence. "The unconscious" of the Zen master is more logical or epistemological than psychological; it is a sort of undifferentiated knowledge, or knowledge of non-distinction, or transcendental Prajna-knowledge.

In Buddhism generally two forms of knowledge are distinguished; the one is *prajna* and the other is *vijnana*. Prajna is all-knowledge (*sarvajna*), or transcendental knowledge, i.e. knowledge undifferentiated. Vijnana is our relative knowledge in which subject and object are distinguishable, including both knowledge of concrete particular things and that of the abstract and universal. Prajna underlies all Vijnana, but Vijnana is not conscious of Prajna and always thinks it is sufficient in itself and with itself, having no need for Prajna. But it is not from Vijnana, relative knowledge, that we get spiritual satisfaction. However much of Vijnana we may accumulate, we can never find our abode of rest in it, for we somehow feel something missing in the inmost part of our being, which science and philosophy can never appease.

Science and philosophy do not apparently exhaust Reality; Reality contains more things than that which is taken up by our relative knowledge for its investigation. What is still left in Reality, according to Buddhism, turns towards Prajna for its recognition. Prajna corresponds to "unconscious consciousness" already referred to. Our spiritual yearnings are never completely satisfied unless this Prajna or unconscious knowledge is awakened, whereby the whole field of consciousness is exposed, inside and outside, to our full view. Reality has now nothing to hide from us.

The Zen master's life-efforts are concentrated in awakening this Prajna, unconscious consciousness, knowledge of non-distinction, which, like a vision of will-o'-the-wisp, unobtrusively, tantalizingly, and constantly shoots through the mind. You try to catch it, to examine it on your palm, to name it definitely, so that you can refer to it as a definitely determined individual object. But this is impossible because it is not an object of dualistically-disposed intellectual treatment. Hence Seppo's "What is this?" and Gensha's more conceptual "Originally Pure."

"This" is not, however, that dark consciousness of the brute or child which is waiting for development and clarification. It is, on the contrary, that form of consciousness which we can attain only after years of hard seeking and hard thinking. The thinking, again, is not to be confused with mere intellection; for it must be, to use the terminology of Kierkegaard, existential thinking and not dialectical reasoning. The Zen consciousness thus realized is the highest form of consciousness. Seppo's following sermon must be appreciated from this point of view:

Seppo appeared in the Dharma-Hall and, seeing the monks who had been waiting long for his discourse, said: "O monks, the bell is struck, and the drum is beaten, and you are gathered here; but what is it that you are seeking for? What ailments have you been suffering? Do you know what shame means? What faults have you ever committed? As I notice, there are only a few of you who have arrived at the goal. Seeing this fact, I could not help coming out and saying to you, 'What is this?' O monks, as soon as you enter the gate I have already finished my interview with you (on this subject). Do you understand? If you do, much labour is saved. Do not, therefore, come to me and try to get something out of my mouth. Do you see?"

The master paused for a while and resumed:

"Even all the Buddhas of the past, present, and future cannot announce it; the books of twelve divisions cannot convey it. How then could those who want to lick the old master's shoes have an understanding on the subject? I say to you, 'What is this?' and you come forward to gather up whatever drops from my lips. If so, you will never have an inkling of it till the year of the ass. I say all this because I cannot help it. But when I say this, I have already committed myself to a downright deception. . . ."

A monk asked, "How does a simple-minded man pass his days?"

"Drinking tea, eating rice."

"Is this not passing time idly?"

"Yes, passing time idly."

"How can one pass time which is not idly?" the monk went on.

The master said, "What's that?"

This "What's that?" is all the time kept busy, has no time to lie idly, but at the same time passes time leisurely as if no divisible time concerned it, because the speaker is ever enjoying "the still point of the turning world". A monk asked, "All things are reducible to the One, but where does the One go?" The master said, "The cowhide-bound skull!" and continued: "If there really be this person (who knows the One), he is worth more than all the gold we could offer him piled from earth to sky. Who says that he is dressed half-naked and just sustains himself?" So saying, he abruptly exclaimed, "What is this?"

Seppo's "What is this?" is the Absolute Present in which time and space are merged as one, as a body of self-identity. Another of his sermons runs thus:

"This understanding does not issue from the lips, from yellow scrolls, from the Zen master's quarters. You should apply yourselves deliberately and find out when you can come across this. If you fail to catch it in this present moment, you will not get it, however many times you are reborn in hundreds of thousands of kalpas. If you want to know what eternity means, it is no further than this very moment. What is this moment? Do not keep on running wild. Your life may soon come to an end. . . ."

It may not be amiss in this connection to cite some
more of Seppo's mondo in order to see how his satori
worked in dealing with the various questions brought to
him by his monks. The questions may not appear appropriate from our modern, logically-attained point of view;
but we must remember that with Zen people nothing is
trivial; everything, including the smallest incidents of our
daily experience, is a matter of grave concern; for even
the lifting of a finger, or the opening of the mouth, the
eyebrows raised, or the shepherd singing is pregnant with
Zen significance.

Question: "What is our daily life?"

The master raised his *hossu*.[1]

The monk went on, "Is this what it is?"

The master said, "What is this?"

No answer came from the monk.

"What is the present moment?"

"I never had a person who asked such a question."

"I am asking you now, master."

The master called aloud, "O you mind-losing fellow!"

"What is the personality of the old master?"

"I have never met any."

"How is it that you never have?"

"Where do you expect to see him?"

The monk did not answer.

"What is there beyond words?"

"What do you seek there?"

"I am asking you now."

"I thought you were quite a clever fellow, but I find
you have all the time been a dull-head."

"What is the most fundamental of fundamentals?"

"Where did you get the idea?"

"If there were any idea of it, it could not be the most
fundamental of fundamentals?"

"What is it then?"

[1] *Hossu* was originally used in India for driving mosquitoes away. It is a
kind of duster with a long tuft of horse's or yak's tail. Now it is a religious
implement.

The monk made no answer. Thereupon the master said, "You ask and I will answer."

The monk asked. The master made him take off his monk-robe, and after beating him several times chased him out of the monastery.

"When one tries to get at it, it flies one thousand miles away. What can one do with it?"

"One thousand miles!"

"What shall I do when the ancient frontier-gate does not turn?"

"Has it turned yet, or not?"

"No turning yet."

"Better have it turned."

"I understand this is your saying: 'There is a thing that will save people in a quiet way, but unfortunately they do not know.' May I ask what this is that quietly saves people?"

"How could you know it?" (You couldn't know it.)

"I heard you say this: 'A room ten feet square contains it.' Now what is that?"

"When you come out of the room, we may consider it."

"Where is it this very moment?"

"Have you come out of the room, or not yet?"

"What (shall I do) when I plan to go back to my native place?"

"Where are you this very moment?"

The monk gave no answer.

"According to the ancient master, when you return to the root, you understand. Now what is the root?"

"The radish-root, the cucumber-root."

"What does it mean when they say, 'Follow forms and you lose the essence'?"

"Lost!"

"It is said that wherever we look around, we hit upon Enlightenment. What does this mean?"

"This is a fine post."

At the end of the summer session, the master (Seppo) sat in front of the monks' quarters. Seeing the monks gathering about him, he raised his staff and said, "This *mine* is meant for people of the second and third grades." A monk asked, "What would you do if the first grade one should turn up?" The master lost no time in striking him.

When Gako, one of Seppo's disciples, became keeper of a small temple, a certain government official came to see him. Noticing a *hossu*, the official took it up and said, "I call this a *hossu*, but what would you call it?" Gako said, "It is not to be called a *hossu*." The officer said, "There are so many Zen masters nowadays noted for their wisdom. Why don't you start on your pilgrimage?" Gako, realizing his incompetence, left his temple and came to Seppo. The latter took him in and said, "How is it that you are here again?" Gako told him about his interview with the government officer whom he failed to satisfy. Seppo said, "Ask me then." Gako repeated the story, whereupon the master uttered the verdict, "A *hossu*!"

"The master of Sai-in is dead. Where is he bound for?"

"It is not you alone but the entire world who know not where he's bound for."

When Seppo saw Gensha, one of his best disciples, he said, "When Jinso the teacher died, a monk came to me and asked, 'Where will he be gone?' I said, 'It is like ice melting into water.'" Gensha replied, "I would not say so." Seppo said, "What would you say?" Gensha said, "It is like water returning to water."

When Kakwan had his first Zen interview with Seppo, Seppo said, "Come nearer." So he advanced and made a bow. The master without saying a word raised his leg and stepped on the prostrate monk. This made the monk suddenly come to a realization. Later, when he made his abode at the Horinho in the Nangaku mountains, he said: "When I was with Seppo I was given a kick by the master, and ever since my eyes are not opened. I wonder what kind of satori it is."

Let me ask, why this remark by Kakwan who evidently had satori under Seppo's foot? Is to *satoru* not to *satoru*? Is to know not to know? Is to be free and master of oneself not to be free and master of oneself? Are affirmations and negations self-identical? Does satori consist in sitting quiet and doing nothing? If you do something, that is, if you act at all, you commit yourself to one thing or another, to a negation or to an affirmation. Does this mean going out of satori and losing it? Is this just sitting quiet, really doing nothing? Is not this doing nothing also doing something? Death itself is doing something. There is no such thing as pure negation, for a negation leads to another negation or to an affirmation— they are mutually conditioning. Satori is indeed beyond all logical analysis.

A monk arrived at Seppo and the master asked, "Where do you come from?"

"I come from Isan."

"What has Isan to say?"

The monk said: "When I was there, I asked him about the meaning of the First Patriarch's coming from the west (over to China). But he kept on sitting in silence."

"Did you approve of it, or not?"

"No, I did not."

Seppo said, "Isan is an 'old Buddha' (meaning great master); you go straight back to him and confess your fault."

Reikwan Osho always kept his gate closed, and sat by himself in meditation. One day Seppo thought of calling on him. He knocked at the gate. Kwan came out and opened it. Seppo lost no time in taking hold of him and demanded, "Is this a simpleton or a sage?" Kwan, spitting, said, "This impish fellow!" and releasing himself from the grip pushed him out and shut the gate again. Seppo said, "It is not in vain to find out what kind of man he is!"

VIII

Now, I think, we can fairly well characterize what Zen satori is:

It is to be with God before he cried out, "Let there be light."

It is to be with God when his spirit moved to give this order.

It is to be with God and also with the light so created.

It is even to be God himself, and also to be his firmament, his earth, his day and night.

Satori is God's coming to self-consciousness in man— the consciousness all the time underlining human consciousness, which may be called super-consciousness.

Satori is not knowledge in its commonly understood sense.

Satori goes beyond knowledge. It is absolute knowledge in the sense that in satori there is neither the knowledge of subject nor the object of knowledge.

Satori is not a higher unity in which two contradictory terms are synthesized. When a staff is not a staff and yet it is a staff, satori obtains.

When the bridge flows and the water does not, there is satori.

Satori is not an act of intuition as long as there are traces in it of a dualistic conception.

Satori is intuition dynamically conceived. When you move with a moving object, when you are identified with it, and yet when you are not moving at all, a certain state of consciousness—super-consciousness—prevails, which is satori.

When an individual monad is perceived reflecting eternity or as eternity itself, there is satori.

Every moment we live is, therefore, eternity itself. Eternity is no other than this instant. They are mutually merged and identical. This state of perfect interpenetration is the content of satori.

Satori does not perceive eternity as stretching itself over an infinite number of unit-instants but in the instant itself, for every instant is eternity.

Satori may be defined as dynamic intuition.

Psychologically speaking, satori is super-consciousness, or consciousness of the Unconscious. The Unconscious is, however, not to be identified with the one psychologically postulated. The Unconscious of satori is with God even prior to his creation. It is what lies at the basis of reality; it is the cosmic Unconscious.

This Unconscious is a metaphysical concept, and it is through satori that we become conscious of the Unconscious.

Satori is Ummon's light possessed by each one of us. And as he says, when we want to lay hands on it there is utter darkness. Satori refuses to be brought on to the surface of our relative consciousness. This, however, does not mean that satori is altogether isolated. To *satoru* means to become conscious of the Unconscious, and this Unconscious is all the time along with consciousness.

Satori makes the Unconscious articulate. And the articulated Unconscious expresses itself in terms of logic incoherently, but most eloquently from the Zen point of view. This "incoherency", indeed, is Zen.

The cosmic Unconscious in terms of space is "Emptiness" (*sunyata*). To reach this Emptiness is satori. Therefore, when things are surveyed from the satori point of view, Mount Sumeru conceals itself in one of the innumerable pores on the skin. I lift a finger and it covers the whole universe.

IV

APPROACHES TO SATORI

I

BROADLY stated, there are two approaches to satori: the one may be termed metaphysical or philosophical or intellectual, and the other psychological or conative. Both start from a certain indefinable spiritual anguish which is harassing enough to make one catch at whatever piece of straw is nearest. This straw may happen to be intellectual or ethical or emotional according to one's predominant trait of character, and also to the environmental factors which are probably working unconsciously.

The philosopher is pre-eminently intellectual, and "religious" people, so-called, are mostly emotional and ethical. We are all to a certain degree the philosopher, the scientist, the moralist, and also spiritually disposed. But most of us are not very strongly inclined to become specifically either one of them. We cannot all be philosophers, but some of us like to approach great problems of life with a more or less intellectual frame of mind. While such persons are not able to pursue the problems with sufficient vigour and logical acumen, they anyway start along this line. With more emotional people the procedure is different; they seek at once a religious leader and listen to his advice. They do not reason very much, they just feel that they must do something to save themselves, otherwise their fall is imminent. Such have no time to use their reason legitimately and patiently. They become devotional followers of Buddha.

Those who come to Zen are generally intellectually inclined. This does not necessarily mean that they are always ready to appeal to their reasoning faculty. They are rather inclined to be intuitive along with their rationalism. They are partly logical; that is, they like to go on reasoning about things they do not understand, but their intellectual will, so to speak, is not so strong as to make them professional philosophers.

In the meantime others prefer a short cut to the final solution. Their intuition is more active than their intellection, and they have reason for this, for they think intuition is more fundamental and a readier instrument to apprehend the truth. They are not satisfied with logical analysis or dialectical proceedings, for these are more concerned with concepts and abstractions, which are not realities. Their interest, on the contrary, is in coming directly in contact with concrete facts. Their intellect is probably strong enough, but they are not predisposed to rely upon it solely. They recognize, though dimly, that often, if not judiciously employed, it leads one to a wrong path which keeps one for ever away from the reality. They are intellectual, we will say, to the extent that they are not a ready prey to the will to believe, especially to blandly believing in anything which has a certain emotional attraction for them.

When we examine biographical records of those prominent Zen masters as entered, however shortly, in *The Transmission of the Lamp*,[1] we notice that most of them were students of the Buddhist Sutras and discourses, of the Confucian classics or Laotzean writings. They could not be satisfied with studying these teachings along the intellectual line. They wished to find out if possible some shorter and surer method of reaching the goal.

[1] *The Transmission of the Lamp* is one of the most important books for students of Zen Buddhism. It was compiled by Dogen (Tao-yuan) of the Eastern Wu, in 1004, in the earlier Sung Dynasty. It contains in its thirty fascicules the history of Zen as beginning with the Seven Buddhas of the past, its introduction to China by Bodhi-Dharma in the Six Dynasties, through successive masters down to the beginning of the Sung Era. What makes the book valuable is its record of mondo, sayings, sermons, and other items left by successive masters of note. Its historical treatment, especially of the "patriarchs" prior to Yeno, now traditionally regarded as the Sixth Patriarch, is not "historical", and requires a thorough overhauling in the light of the T'ung Huang materials. The author of this book has handled the subject in his forthcoming studies in the early history of Zen thought in China.

One of the most notable examples is Tokusan, who was a great student of the *Diamond Sutra*. His understanding of it was mainly intellectual. When he heard of Zen, he could not believe it; but he must have felt a certain uneasiness about himself. Though he was not definitely conscious of it, he must have felt some yearning for Zen. Superficially he opposed it and wished to defeat it if he could. Shido spent more than ten years in the pursuit of the *Nirvana Sutra*, and finally came to Yeno, the Sixth Patriarch, to be enlightened about it. There was one passage which he found particularly difficult. The Sutra said that when you go beyond birth-and-death there will be absolute tranquillity, which is the supreme bliss. But Shido could not understand who will enjoy such bliss, when this relative world of birth-and-death is altogether destroyed, and when there is nobody left for anything in the absolute emptiness of things.

This was the way he reasoned about Nirvana, which he took for absolute annihilation. Yeno explained that Shido was not yet free from the bonds of relativity and intellectual thinking. He said: "This very 'moment' is not subject to birth-and-death, and therefore there is no going beyond them as long as we live this present moment. Here is absolute tranquillity which is no other than this present moment. Bliss lies in the timelessness of this present moment. There is here no particular recipient of their bliss and, therefore, every one of us is blessed with eternal bliss. . . ."

Some may say that this is a highly abstract reasoning. But their judgement is the outcome of intellectual deliberation and rationalistic thinking; from the Zen point of view Yeno's statement is a direct communication out of his inner perception. He is living this Eternal Now where he sees, as a fact of his personal experience, that no such things as birth-and-death exist. This information was what Shido was after.

When I say that Zen followers are intellectually inclined, I mean that they are not satisfied with intellection after their trial with it, and wish to discover a more direct way of dealing with realities. From whatever motives and in whatever environmental conditions they approach Zen, they all expect Zen to give the most dependable eye-witness-like information in regard to ultimate truth, which will relieve them completely of all kinds of mental vexations and also of dialectical complications.

That Zen attracts people intellectually predisposed is inevitable, seeing that satori is the way to get them out of the impasse in which they are sure to find themselves while they keep on their rationalistic course of study. The intellect is primarily intended to enable us to get on well with a world dualistically conceived; but for probing into ultimate reality it is an inadequate instrument, and for this we have gone through enough spiritual suffering. Zen claims to save us from this, and the fact of salvation has been demonstrated fully, as we read in the annals of Zen.

II

There are two main currents in Buddhism, intellectual and devotional. The devotional element has expressed itself in the Pure Land school of China and Japan, while the intellectual element has found its fullest development in such teachings as Nagarjuna's and Vasubhandu's and Asanga's in the fifth and the sixth century in India. Nagarjuna's school marks the culmination of the Sunyata idea (Emptiness) as expressed in the Mahayana sutras, whereas Asanga's and Vasubhandu's is the idealistic psychological school based on the theory of Vijnapti-matra (representations only). Both of them, Nagarjuna's and Asanga-Vasubhandu's schools, have pushed their speculations to their utmost ends, so that no further development could be expected of them. Besides, they have gone too far away from the proper sphere of religious thought. If Buddhism were to live as a religious teaching, it had to be transplanted somewhere else. Indian thought had exhausted her fertility to give any more nourishment to the growth of Buddhism as religion.

Fortunately, it so happened that Bodhi-Dharma came to China early in the sixth century to make a fresh start for Buddhism in a soil where a more pragmatically minded people had been waiting for it. In the beginning, the Chinese revolted against the Indian mind because they were diametrically opposed. The Indian mind excelled in speculation while the Chinese was pre-eminently practical. But after some years of struggle they came to understand each other, and the result was the growth of Zen school of Buddhism in China.

While the Indian mind soared high in the air and lived among the stars, the Chinese always remembered that they could not get away from the earth where they had their start. When a Zen master was talking with a Buddhist scholar whose mind was still deeply saturated with the Indian way of abstract reasoning, the topic of discussion turned to Suchness; the master declared that the teacher failed to grasp the idea of Suchness, for the teacher did not know what Tathagatahood meant. The teacher asked, "What is the meaning of it then?"

M.: "*Tathagata* means that all things are such (*tatha*) as they are."

T.: "That is right, the *tathagata* means the suchness of all things."

M.: "But your affirmation is not quite up to the mark."

T.: "Is this not what is declared in the sutras?"

M.: "Let me ask you: Are you of suchness?"

T.: "Yes, I am."

M.: "Are the trees and stones of suchness?"

T.: "Yes, they are."

M.: "Is your suchness the same as the suchness of trees and stones?"

T.: "They are not different."

M.: "But how different you are from trees and stones."

As we see here, the one is thinking in abstractions, losing touch with concrete realities, while the other is dealing with sense-facts of experience as they confront us. Zen refuses to be carried away from our daily experiences, though it recognizes a value not to be derived

from mere sense-data. Someone asks what the Buddha is
—he evidently had some exalted notion of a super-
natural being—and Zen answers, "Pick out what is not
Buddha and show it to me right here." When Amida's
parentage comes up in question, Zen at once declares,
"His family name is Kaushika,[1] and his mother's
Beautifully-faced."

Zen is always ready to give an answer to any question
with which those erudite scholars of Buddhism may
attempt to baffle the master.

The one strong point which Zen has over the recondite
scholarship of Buddhists is that the masters are always
sure of their ground, and can hold it against anything
coming from the other camp. The latter tries to be
logical and common-sense and consistent, but Zen does
not follow the routine of reasoning, and does not mind
contradicting itself or being inconsistent. The two are
walking on different planes of consciousness. The satori
plane can never be reached by the rationalistic plane,
however ingeniously it may be handled. For there is a
gap between the two planes, and in order to cross it an
"existential leap", as Kierkegaard calls it, is required,
whereas the satori plane, when it is once attained, is
always interfused with the intellectual. For this reason,
scholarship is quite helpless against satori, for the master
knows where the scholars are, but the latter are just
groping in the dark to locate themselves.

Doko was a great scholar of the Vijnapti-matra school
of Buddhism; this school assumes the existence of many
forms of consciousness or minds, each of which is assigned
to a definite task in one's mental activities. Hence this
question put by Doko to Daishu, the Zen master:

"By means of which mind does the Zen master discipline himself in the Way?"

Daishu replied, "I have no mind to make use of, nor
is there any Way in which to discipline myself."

"If there is no mind to make use of, nor any Way in

[1] Kaushika is the name of Indra while he was still a human being.
Here it can be anything, Mason or Johnson.

which to discipline oneself, how is it that you have such a large following who are devoted to the study of Zen and discipline themselves in the Way?"

"When I have not an inch of ground even as large as the point of a drill, where can I house the large following you speak of? When I have no tongue, how can I persuade them to follow me?"

"How can a Zen master tell a lie to one's face?"

"When I have no tongue to persuade others, how can I tell a lie?"

"I utterly fail to understand you," said Doko, the scholar.

"I myself am unable to understand," replied Daishu, the master.

The purpose of the Zen master's flatly contradicting facts of sense-experience is to persuade the psychologist to free himself from undue attachment to concepts which he takes for realities. The Zen master has by his satori attained a vantage-ground from which he sallies out to attack the opponent's camp in any direction. This vantage-ground is not located at any definite point of space, and cannot be assailed by concepts or any system based on them. His position, which is not a position in its ordinary sense, cannot, therefore, be overtaken by any means born of intellection.

The psychologist, philosopher, or theologian of any hue falls short of catching him out at his work, for as he does not mind contradicting himself, he is "out of bounds" to any rational argument. Daishu denied he had a mouth, and yet with this non-existent mouth of his he insisted that he could not tell a lie.

There was another master who was concerned very much with the mouth without which his questioner could not feed himself. A monk asked Ho-un of Rosozan:

"What is the meaning of 'Words are uttered and yet no words are uttered?' "

Ho-un said, "Where is your mouth?"

The monk replied, "I have no mouth."

"How do you eat then?" demanded the master.

As the monk failed to see the point, Ho-un later gave his answer for the monk, "He never feels hungry and there is no need for him to eat."

Let me cite another mondo about the mouth. Yakusan Igen (751–834), a disciple of Sekito Kisen, seeing a monk-gardener planting vegetables, said to him, "There is nothing to say against your planting, but do not let the vegetables strike root."

The monk replied, "If they do not strike root, what would our brotherhood eat?"

Yakusan queried, "Have you a mouth or not?"

The monk did not answer.

All these inconsistencies and irrationalities of the Zen masters are in fact their strong point. As they are so absolutely sure of the position gained from their experience, they know that they are above logic. Satori has a certain definite quality of being final. When you have it you know within yourself that there is no further way to go on and feel completely satisfied and restful. As this is not to be reached by mere intellection, satori is safe from its interference. On the contrary, logic is now required to take notice of the experience of satori as an irrefutable and almost fundamental fact, and to try to explain it by manœuvring its entire forces. If the system of logic that has been in circulation is found inadequate to explain away the satori experience and mondo that have grown up from it, the philosopher will have to invent a new system of thinking to fit the experience, and not conversely, that is, to disprove the empirical facts by means of abstract logic.

III

Zen also hates externalism inasmuch as it refuses to be other than itself. Externalism knows how to bind people but never does much towards spiritual liberation. Intellectualism is a sort of externalism. Rules of logic warp or maim or suppress even man's highest creative aspirations.

This is unbearable for Zen, as we have already seen in the many instances already cited. We will give now some more instances of Zen masters who revolted against the Vinaya rules of conduct.

The Vinaya rules of conduct are useful and praiseworthy, and when the monks lead their lives in accordance with them they will certainly be good Buddhists and prove to be fine examples for others. But when the Vinaya cannot go further and deeper than merely regulating one's outward behaviour, they will surely become an undesirable impediment to one's spiritual development.

This was the feeling the Zen masters had when they harnessed themselves with the Vinaya rules. Nangaku Ejo, Nansen, Rinzai, Tokusan, and other great figures in the Zen history of the T'ang dynasty were all earnest students of the Vinaya texts, but this never satisfied their inner needs, which was especially the case with Keichin of Rakan-in (867–928). He was one day giving lessons in the Vinaya to a congregation of monks; when he had finished, he conceived the idea that the Vinaya is meant first to regulate our bodily behaviour and is not conducive to spiritual emancipation; that what he wanted could never be attained by merely following words of mouth. So thinking, he quitted his Vinaya and embraced Zen.

Zen aims at emancipation, not only from artificial rules of discipline but from the fetters of ratiocination; in other words, Zen wants to be free from concepts. Man is the only being who creates concepts and thereby manages to handle reality. But concepts never exhaust reality; there always remains something which eludes our conceptual handling. But most of us imagine that we are perfect masters of reality, and try to deceive ourselves that we are really free and happy. This gullibility and self-deception cannot endure, because it appeals only to the superficial part of our consciousness; the deeper nature, temporally hypnotized, is sure to assert itself before long.

And the Zen method of making man really and truly free and emancipated and master of himself is quite radical. Every trace of conceptualism is to be wiped out in a most ruthless manner; what man has hitherto cherished as the last thing to part with must be thrown aside; the most thoroughgoing work of negation is to be accomplished, as negation itself is to be negated until there is absolutely nothing left for negation. This is Nirvana. A Buddhist philosopher asked, "What is Great Nirvana?" Daishu answered, "It is not to commit yourself to the karma of birth-and-death."[1]

"What is the karma of birth-and-death?" asked the philosopher.

"To seek Great Nirvana is the karma of birth-and-death; to give up defilements and to get attached to purities is the karma of birth-and-death; where there is gain and attainment, there is the karma of birth-and-death; not to get rid of thought of opposites is the karma of birth-and-death."

The monk asked, "How do we then attain emancipation?"

"From the first," answered the master, "we have never been in bondage, and therefore there is no need to seek release. Just use (it),[2] just act (it)—this is indeed incomparable."

IV

Zen requests us to negate everything which comes our way, and even this attempt to negate is to be negated. We thus come to a state of absolute nothingness or emptiness. But if we are still conscious of this state we are

---

[1] "The karma of birth-and-death" means "karma that leads to birth-and-death." Buddhists conceive this world of opposites or relativities in terms of birth-and-death, and tell us to rise above this dualism if we desire to be enlightened, free, which is Nirvana.

[2] To apprehend what this "it" is is satori, for "it" is such a fugitive experience as not to be caught up even by the finest network of concepts. It is significant in a way that the Chinese grammar does not require here any pronoun: it simply states, "Just use, just act", and does not specify what to use and who is to act or what to act. The verb has no subject; act, actor, acted—these three are one and the same; and what is this "one and the same" is "it". I have inserted "it" in parentheses.

not yet fully emancipated; there is a residue yet to be cleared off. Indeed, as long as there is the slightest trace of consciousness, we are one thousand miles away from satori. If so, we may ask, how could we ever speak of it?

The mind cannot be reduced to a state of blankness; it can never be a mere piece of wood or brick. But what Zen requires seems to be no more, no less than that. Sometimes the Zen master actually tells us to destroy every bit of human consciousness and be turned into a senseless piece of inorganic matter. This is evidently the climax of irrationality.

But this is exactly where Zen is planning to drive us, for was it not Zen that wanted us to get rid of every intellectual effort to achieve emancipation or attain satori? Such notions as the annihilation of consciousness, the insensibility of inorganic existence, an infinite series of negations, or the unrealizability of absolute emptiness are all products of conceptualism. To approach Zen by this route is to go exactly the opposite way to that prescribed by Zen. Zen will never be attained along this way.

A monk asked Ummon, "Is there any fault when there is not one thought arising?" The master said (as much as), "Mount Sumeru!" Does this not fully demonstrate that Zen abhors the presence of anything even approximating to a concept or "thought"? "From the first," says the master, "we have not been in bondage, and there is nothing from which we are to be released." Being so, even to refer to a negation will be committing a great fault.

A monk came to Joshu, "How is it when I come to you with nothing?"

"Cast it down!" said Joshu.

"What shall I cast down when I have nothing?"

"If so," said Joshu, "take it away!"

As long as we are dealing with concepts we can never come to a conclusion which is really conclusive. A monk asked a master, "Please show me the way without appealing to words of mouth." To this the master gave this answer, "Ask me without using words of mouth."

Yes, concepts are needed to expel concepts, but we ought to know their limits. The Zen mondo seems to be the only way to get us out of this impasse. The point is to see within ourselves, to see into our own being, to become aware of our inmost working which never comes before our consciousness by means of intellection. One may call it an act of intuition, but an intuition suggests the idea of two things facing each other. Would it not be better to call it an event of self-awareness, or going through the experience of self-identity? What Zen does is give one an opportunity to have this experience. It never argues about the possibility of such an experience, or about its desirability or significance, for this is appealing to reasoning, and the reasoning, however convincing as far as it goes, can never be experience itself; it lacks subjectivity, it is after all a form of externalism. The masters are perfectly aware of this, for they have gone through this experience. From the rationalistic point of view, therefore, their retorts, or rejoinders, or counter-charges, or contradictions, or rebutters—whatever their "answers" may be termed— are no answers at all in whatever sense we may take them. They are in reality just meant to turn on the tap of experience for the monk whose desperate efforts to realize his spiritual freedom and emancipation have been completely baffled. Zen being the only passageway left to his inquiring mind, the master's one word or question is often enough to usher the questioner into the secret chamber hitherto closed to him.

When he asks about the meaning of Dharma's idea of coming from the West (that is, the essence of Buddhism), the master simply says, "Whence do you come?" When the question of "the true straightforward Way" comes up, the master's remark is, "The rider on the donkey is searching for the donkey." When the Absolute, where the dualistic opposition of subject and object has never taken place, is made the topic of discussion, the master says, "I had a pretty good memory some time in the past." The monk continued, "How about now?" The master said, "Not only my ears are failing me, but my eyes are growing dimmer."

Bifurcation of reality into subject and object is the work of intellection. When there is no such working, life is a complete whole with no cleavage in it, and with the old master it is altogether a natural thing to become more or less deaf and dim-sighted.

The main point is to become aware of this perfect state of self-identity where all conceptual contradictions are effaced. This awareness is, however, neither psychological nor logical; it is spiritual, so to speak, for there is no one who is aware of something, nor is there something which becomes the object of awareness. Yet there is distinctly a state of awareness which is called satori. Ordinarily this strange thing never turns up as an object of consciousness, yet it never ceases to be in action; indeed every one of us, including the whole universe, i.e. what is known as reality, is no more than this "it", and the object of Zen discipline is to prepare our relative consciousness for it.

One of the Zen masters of the Sung dynasty touched on this in the following discourse: "It is only because all beings are using 'it' in their daily life and yet not conscious of the fact. For instance, all the three thousand chilio-cosms, inclusive of suns and moons, stars and constella-tions, rivers and oceans, the *Wei* and the *Chi* and all the living beings in them, are passing through from one pore of the skin to another, and yet the pores are not gaining in size, nor is the whole cosmos losing its magnitude. In the midst of this (miracle), all beings are not at all aware of the event. Indeed, even when they understand it they go on without being conscious of it (without being logically and psychologically, i.e. differentially conscious of it)."

In spite of all this, we are ever urged by intellectual curiosity to probe into the mystery, although it is really the mystery itself that incites the curiosity. People may think that it is God who made this world with all his sinful children in it, but that being unable to endure their sinning, he devised a means to save them, and that intellection is one of such means. But in fact it is God himself who wished to see himself, and with that end in view created the world with its creatures, the creatures wishing to reach him being his own wish to see himself.

God was curious about himself and created the intellect, but the strangest thing, that goes beyond human reason, is that God ever wished to see himself, and the reason is not the proper instrument for understanding it, though it is able to raise all kinds of questions and put itself in a quandary. This is how intellectually inclined persons come to Zen to find the solution.

v

Let me cite some masters to show how they came to study Zen. Hoyen (–1104) of Gosozan was thirty-five when he was ordained a Buddhist monk. While in Cheng-tu he was devoted to the Vijnapti-matra school of Mahayana Buddhism. There he learned the following story: When the Bodhisattva enters the stage of Insight, his intelligence is united with reason, and what is external is merged into the spirit, and there is no differentiation between the seer and the seen. Some of the Indian philosophers objected: if there is no differentiation between the seer and the seen, who can testify to the fact of seeing? The Buddhist scholar being unable to meet this objection, he was not allowed to strike the bell or to beat the drum to call up his congregation; he was also deprived of wearing the Buddhist robe.

When Genjo Hsuan-tsang (660–664) visited India he was able to save the Buddhist from the situation by saying, "It is like a man drinking water; he knows by himself whether it is cold or hot."

Hoyen thought to himself: "It is all very well to know by oneself whether the water is cold or not, but what is the content of this experience?" He approached the teacher and asked, "How do we get at the fact of self-consciousness?" The teacher could not enlighten him on this point and directed him to see a Zen master.

Later, when Hoyen mastered all the secrets of Zen, he gave this sermon: "Buddhas and Patriarchs are your deadly enemies; satori is nothing but a drabbling with the mind. Rather be a man who does nothing, just leisurely passing his time. Be like a deaf-mute in the world of sounds and colours. But tell me how you would achieve this. To say 'yes' is not right, to say 'no' is not right, to say 'yes' and 'no' is not right, either. But if there should suddenly appear a man who declared, to say 'yes' is all right, to say 'no' is all right, to say 'yes' and 'no' is also all right, what would you tell him? As for me, I say this: I know full well where you are earning your livelihood; it is in the devil's den."

When Hoyen realized that he was about to pass away, he gathered his congregation and gave his farewell sermon: "Joshu the master has his last word, and now how do you understand it? Let me see if there is any one of you who can come forward and say, I do. If you really understand, there is nothing to hinder your being free and lively. But if you say you do not understand yet, how can I explain this happy event?" So saying, Hoyen sat in silence for a while, and continued, "In whatever way I tell you about it and in however conclusive a manner, you will still feel uninformed. Do you see? The rich man does not think one thousand mouths are too many to feed, while the poor man has not enough to look after just one person. Fare you well."

Dosan (807–869) was a great master of the Late T'ang dynasty, and the founder of the school bearing his name. His interest in Zen started with the *Prajna-hridaya-sutra* (*Shingyo* in Japanese), in which he read, "No eye, no ear, no nose, no tongue, no body, and no mind." This troubled him very much. While feeling all over his face with his hands, he thought the scripture could not be right, but how could the Buddha tell a lie? This was when he was still very young, which proves that his mind was philosophically inclined.

It was when he was twenty-one that he had his head

shaved and officially joined the Brotherhood. On his Zen pilgrimage the first master he visited was Nansen (748–834), who was one of the chief disciples of Baso (788). When the latter's death-day was approaching Nansen prepared the usual commemoration dinner for his Brotherhood. He took advantage of the occasion and dropped a question to them, saying, "Tomorrow I am going to offer a special meal to my departed master; do you think he will come back to take it with us?" Nobody answered, but Dosan came forward and said, "He will as soon as he finds a company."

Dosan went next to Isan, wishing to get enlightened on the story of "preaching by non-sentient beings". The story started with Yechu the national teacher (775), a disciple of Yeno, the Sixth Patriarch. The point of the story is "How can a non-sentient being give a discourse on the Dharma?"

Isan said, "We too have it here (that is, we have non-sentient beings constantly discoursing on the Dharma). Only we find it difficult to come across the capable person."

Dosan said, "Pray tell me how."

Isan replied, "It is impossible to tell you with the mouth that was given by our parents."

Dosan then went to Ungan and asked, "When a non-sentient being discourses, who is it that hears it?"

Ungan said, "A non-sentient being's discourse is heard by another non-sentient being."

"Do you hear it, master?" Dosan asked.

"If I hear," said Ungan, "you won't hear my preaching."

"If that is so, Ryokai[1] himself cannot hear the master's discourse?"

"When you fail to hear even my discourse, how much less do you hear a non-sentient being's discourse!" Ungan concluded.

This mondo opened Dosan's mind, and he exclaimed:

[1] Ryokai is Dosan's own name.

How very strange!
How very strange!
The non-sentient's discourse is indeed beyond thought!
When you listen with the ear, you cannot understand;
Let the eye catch the sounds and for the first time you
understand.

This view was endorsed by Ungan, who, however,
cautioned him not to be too hasty. Dosan did not grasp
quite clearly what Ungan meant by this advice. When
Dosan happened to cross a stream, he noticed his own
reflection on the water, and this unexpectedly revealed
to him what Ungan meant by his parting advice. Dosan
composed another stanza:

It is to be scrupulously avoided—the seeking ("him")
in others,
Receding ever further away from me, ("he") is
estranged.
I am going alone this moment all by myself,
And whatever I may be, I meet him.
He is no other than myself,
Yet now I am not he.
It should thus be understood,
For it is then that Suchness is fully testified.

In contrast to Dosan's philosophical frame of mind,
Ryutan Soshin may be said to be practically-minded. He
was teacher of Tokusan (780–865), who was noted for
swinging his staff. When Soshin was still a young village
lad, of a family keeping a bakery shop, he used to take
ten pieces of cake to Tenno Dogo, who was the master
residing in the Zen monastery. Dogo gratefully accepted
them, but always left one piece and gave it to Soshin,
saying, "This is for you with the prayer that your descen-
dants be blessed thereby." Soshin one day happened to
reflect on the matter. "Strange that he should give me
back one of the cakes which I take from my own shop!
Could there be a special meaning?" He finally approached
Dogo with the question, to which the master answered,

"What fault could there be when things you bring are returned to you?"

This seems to have enlightened the lad's mind. He wished to be ordained as a Zen monk, and the name Soshin was given him by the master.

Soshin naturally expected to be instructed in Zen as a school boy is taught at school. But Dogo gave him no special lesson on the subject, which bewildered and disappointed Soshin. One day he said to the master, "It is some time since I came here, but not a word has been given me regarding the essence of the Zen teaching." Dogo replied, "Since your arrival I have ever been giving you lessons on the matter of mental discipline in Zen."

"What kind of lesson could it have been?"

"When you bring me a cup of tea in the morning, I take it from you; when you serve me a meal I accept it; when you bow to me I return it with a nod. Where else do you expect to be taught the mental discipline of Zen?"

Soshin hung his head for a while, pondering the puzzling words of the master. The master said, "If you want to see, see right at once. When you begin to think, you miss the point."

Soshin now got into the meaning of Dogo's remark, and asked, "How shall I take care of it?"

"Just go on at your ease as Nature dictates; don't feel restrained but move along in accordance with the circumstances (in which you happen to find yourself). The only thing needed is to purge all your vulgar thoughts; there is no specifically superior understanding."

("Vulgar thoughts" means thoughts or imaginations or anything else that are based on the dualistic view of reality. When these are purged, there arises by itself what might be called a "superior understanding", which is satori.)

Soshin later had his residence at Ryutan in Reishu (Li-chou). Ryutan means "Dragon's Pool". When Tokusan visited him, he said, "I have heard people talk so much about Dragon's Pool. Now that I am here, I see no pool, no dragon." Soshin said, "You are right in the Dragon's Pool!" Tokusan remained quiet. Later, a master by the name of Genkaku commented: "Tell me whether Tokusan approves Soshin or not. If he gave Soshin his approval, what did he see here? If he did not, why did he become Soshin's successor?"

Tokusan, before he came to Ryutan, was a great student of the *Diamond Sutra* as was already noted, but after his conversion he did not indulge any more in discoursing on Prajna. His favourite method of dealing with Zen students was "thirty blows" regardless of their saying "yes" or "no" to his question. One dictum he left for posterity sums up the essence of the practical teaching of Zen: "Be business-less in mind, be mind-less in business."

This requires some explanation. The original Chinese runs thus: "*wu shih yu hsin, wu hsin yu shih*". "Business" is not used here in its ordinary sense. *Shih* in fact means "affairs", "event", "happening", "fact", "occurrence", etc.; and "be business-less" is made here to mean "not to be concerned with", "not to be bothered about", "to act as if not acting", "to live taking no thought of the morrow", "to grow like the lilies of the field, to work like the fowls of the air". The wind blows, branches bend, the flowers are scattered, but the wind has never had any ill will, nor do the trees harbour any feeling of enmity. "To be business-less in mind," therefore, means to be like the wind blowing, the trees bending, the flowers blooming, the birds singing, which is to say, to have the mind purged of concupiscence, self-centred thoughts, power-thirsty feelings.

Man is a conscious judging being, and gives values to everything which comes his way. He may do anything he likes according to his sweet will or to his capricious judgement, but at the same time there is something in him which makes him confess with Paul (Rom. viii, 20): "The good that I would I do not; but the evil which I would not, that I do."

This wretched helplessness which Paul ascribes to the

carnal body of death is a contradiction which all of us humans harbour within ourselves, and as long as we judge things by moral and rational standards we cannot get out of the contradiction. This is great spiritual tribulation, and, in the terminology of the Zen masters, is the "business" upsetting the mind. "To be business-less", therefore, means to be free from the captivity of intellection and moralization.

"Be mind-less in business" is the reverse of the first injunction, which is here objectively translated. "Business" is our daily life, and "to have no mind" is to be free from selfish calculation, to be "delighted in the law of God after the inward man" (Rom. viii, 22). Paul's "inward man" corresponds to Tokusan's "mindlessness". To have a fine mind is a good thing, for you will be successful in the world. But this will never help you to get into the spiritual realm where real happiness abides. But when you are "mindless" in all your dealings and doings, in all the "business" which constitutes our worldly life, you live a purposeless life not filled with "hopes that are seen", but with hopes "that we see not".

The Zen-man who would live a "mindless", "business-less", purposeless life is one of those "that love God, who are the called according to God's purposes" (Rom. viii, 24, 28), and let me remind you, not to man's purpose. To use more Christian terms, "to be mindless and businessless" is to be without "the carnal mind", "to be spiritually minded which is peace and life". To be mindless may be taken as meaning purely natural, or mechanically purposeless, but the idea the Zen master wishes to express by mindlessness is innocently and egolessly receiving the will of "the Father which sent me".

To be spiritually-minded may mean to "take no thought for your life what ye shall eat, or what ye shall drink; nor yet for your body, what ye shall put on". (Matt. vi, 25). But with some Zen masters eating and being clothed is just as important as devoting oneself to spiritual discipline. For even "the carnal body" is to be well taken care of when we know from our actual experience that without the body no spirit can exist, although this does not necessarily mean that the body comes first at the expense of the spirit, as maintained by the materialists.

The truth is that there is no matter apart from the spirit and no spirit apart from matter, and that to take care of the one is to take care of the other, and, therefore, that while attending to the one, the other is never to be neglected or ignored or put altogether aside. Zen's position, properly stated, is always advaitistic, which means neither two nor one, but two in one and one in two. Ho-koji, who was the noted lay-disciple of Baso in the Middle T'ang Dynasty once wrote:

> Miraculous deeds and acts of wonder . . .
> I carry water, I fetch kindling.

Umpo Bunyetsu was a disciple of Daigu Shushi of the Early Sung Dynasty. When he first visited his master, he heard him saying to his Brotherhood: "When you are gathered here you eat vegetable salad; (now pick up a stalk and) if you call it a stalk, you go to hell as fast as a flying arrow." Bunyetsu was taken aback, and in the evening he went to the master. The master said, "What do you want here?" Yetsu expressed his wish to be instructed in the mental discipline. Daigu, however, told him to look after the provisions, for he said, "You are yet young and strong; why not go out and beg food for the Brotherhood? When I am busy fighting hunger, how should I talk to you about Zen?"

Yetsu humbly obeyed the master's admonition and spent his time in begging food. After a while the master was transferred to another monastery at Suigan. Yetsu followed him. When one day he asked the master again for instruction, the master said, "Buddha's Dharma is not yet rotten to the core; as it is snowing and cold, you had better go out and gather charcoal for the Brotherhood." Yetsu obediently carried out the mission as told, and duly

reported, when the master again gave him other work:
"The overseer's position is vacant, and I wish you would
take it up for yourself."

Yetsu was not at all pleased with the request of the
master, whom he thought unduly unsympathetic. One
day while he was washing himself at the rear of the
dormitory, the bands of the basket got loose, which caused
the shelf to fall. The incident unexpectedly opened his
mind to satori. He hurriedly put on his regular monk's
robe and called on the master. The master was greatly
pleased to see him, saying, "How happy I am to see you
thus finishing the great work!" Yetsu simply made bows
and departed without uttering a word. He stayed with the
master for eight years after this, until finally he succeeded
the master as abbot of the Suigan monastery.

VI

Gensha Shibi once said to his monks: "It is like being
deeply immersed in the great ocean; the waves are over
your head, yet you do not stop stretching your arms and
pitifully ask for water." Zen is like this, and we who
talk about various approaches to it are doing much for
nothing. But the thing we can never understand is that
we are so constituted as to be ever curious about discovering what we are and where we are and why. To
satisfy this curiosity, Gensha further tells us the qualities
needed.

"I tell you, those Bodhisattvas who wish to study
Prajna ought to be endowed with great character and
great intelligence. If your natural powers are dull and
not quick enough, you have to be hard-working day and
night, putting out the best that lies in you. Waste not your
time in just memorizing words and phrases. If you do,
you will not know what to do when someone comes and
asks you (about Zen). . . ."

Whatever Gensha meant by "great character" (*dai
kon-ki*), and "great intelligence" (*dai chi-ye*), it is certain

that the study of Zen requires a great intellectual integrity and strength of character. The persistent pursuit of one task is no easy business, especially when this involves the disregarding of worldly affairs. But unless it is sustained by great spiritual aspirations, the study of Zen will be impossible.

First comes the awakening of "great intelligence", which makes us wonder what it is that acquaints us with the presence of the great ocean while we ourselves are deeply immersed in it. This separation of ourselves from the all-embracing, all-submerging "ocean" is the function of the intelligence, for it is because of this that we crave for the water of life. Here lies the great spiritual tragedy of man; the water of life is desired, and this water surrounds him, soaks him, enters into every fibre and every cell of his tissues, is indeed himself, and yet he does not realize it and seeks it outside himself, even beyond the "great ocean".

The intelligence is a great mischief-worker, and yet without it we shall never be able to wake up the greater one. It separates us from the ocean in which we live; if not for this separation we should be found forever slumbering under the waves, blind and ignorant. The only trouble is, as Gensha says, that we look for "the great ocean" in words, concepts, and their various combinations, and the result is that we know nothing, understand nothing, and when people ask for help we completely fail to satisfy them, saying nothing about our own spiritual realization.

The case of a Zen master endowed with "great character" and "great intelligence" is found in Bankei (1622–1693) who lived in the earlier part of the Tokugawa Era. His career may be regarded as typifying the Zen discipline in the pre-koan period, and designated as the metaphysical approach to Zen.

He was born in a Samurai family. His father was Suga Dosetsu, a Confucian, who at the time lived in Hamada, Isai country, in the prefecture of Harima. Bankei was a strong personality from childhood. He disliked just learning calligraphy and reading the Chinese classics, as taught in those days, and he used to leave his school before the lessons were over. His elder brother, who was the head of the family since the father's death, which took place when Bankei was ten years old, worried over Bankei's wilfulness. To prevent his early departure from school, he instructed the ferryman not to take him in the boat when he came to the river which he had to cross on his way home.

Bankei, however, was not to be dismayed. He said, "The ground continues under the water, and I can walk." He plunged into the river, and swam under the stream, finally managing to land on the other side.

In those days boys used to play a mimic battle, taking position on both banks of the river and throwing stones at each other, and it is said that whichever side Bankei took was sure to win, for the simple reason that he would not beat retreat until a final victory was gained.

Bankei could not get on well with his elder brother, who, being apparently a vigorous disciplinarian and conventional in his way of thinking, could not probe into Bankei's deeper nature. This depressed the young Bankei very much. One day he decided to commit suicide to avoid further conflicts with the brother. He swallowed a large number of spiders, as he remembered people talking about their being poisonous. Then he shut himself up in a small Buddhist shrine and sat quietly waiting for death. But this did not take place. Perhaps in the meantime he thought the matter over and came out of the shrine, or perhaps his family, noticing his long absence, hunted him out after a thorough search.

These incidents must have taken place before he was twelve, when he began to study *Great Learning*, one of the Confucian classics, very likely under another teacher than the last to whom his brother had sent him. Bankei was greatly troubled with the sentence: "The way of Great Learning is to brighten up the Bright Virtue." What is the Bright Virtue? He wanted to know. The teacher exhausted his learning to make it clear to him, but this could not satisfy him, because what he wanted was not any amount of definitions and explanations, but the substance itself. This doubt led him to the study of Zen. The following is his own account of his spiritual adventure:

"My father was a *ronin*[1] formerly living in the Shikoku, and a Confucian. I was born after my family moved to this district.[2] Father died when I was still young, and I was brought up by mother. I was quite unruly in my younger days, mother tells me, and becoming the leader of other unruly youngsters did a great deal of mischief. But ever since I was two or three years old I seem to have unusually disliked the event known as death, and when I cried aloud without cause they imitated the dead or talked about death, which at once stopped my crying and kept me from getting people into further trouble.

"When I grew up, mother sent me to a teacher in Chinese and made me learn how to read the texts. In those days Confucianism flourished in this part of the country. When we came to the section in the *Great Learning* which treats of the Bright Virtue,[3] saying that the Way of Great Learning was to brighten up the Bright Virtue, I could not get the meaning of the dictum, 'What is the Bright Virtue?' I could find no way through.

"My doubt was not to be readily dissolved. I went among Confucian scholars asking 'What is the Bright Virtue?' 'What does it look like?' But none of them could enlighten me on the subject, and said that such a question was hard for them to deal with and that it was better for me to go to a Zen master who might be able to tell what's what. They said, further, that their business chiefly consisted in reading books on the Confucian teaching and explaining the literal meaning of the words in which it was expressed, and that as to the Bright Virtue itself they

---

[1] A *ronin* was a Samurai who was not attached to any feudal lord.

[2] Hamada in the province of Harima, where a friend of his younger days built a fine temple for him.

[3] *Mei-toku*. *Mei* means "bright", "clear", "illuminating", and *teh* is "virtue".

had no knowledge whatever. This was disappointing. I made up my mind to visit a Zen master, but in those days there were no Zen temples round here.

"I was, however, firmly determined to find out what this Bright Virtue was. I was also determined to make my aged mother acquainted with it before her day to pass away should come. Wishing to get through with this problem, I made use of every opportunity. I attended whatever Buddhist sermons and discourses were given and was also present at every such meeting I heard about. On my return from such meetings I would tell my mother everything I had learned there. But after all these wanderings my knowledge of the Bright Virtue did not make any headway whatever.

"Finally I made up my mind to find a Zen master. Finding one, I visited him, and asked about the Bright Virtue. He told me to practise Zazen[1] if I wanted to know what it was. Now I took up Zazen. Going up the mountains and into a cave discovered there, I went in and sat with my seat bared, not minding how rugged the rock was. I often kept up my Zazen for seven days on end without eating. Once seated I gave myself up to it regardless of what might come, even risking my life for it. I often kept on sitting cross-legged until I fell from the rock exhausted. As there was nobody to bring me things to eat, my fasting went on for days on end.

"After such austerities (which did not bring any result) I came back to my native village, where I had a little hut built, and shut myself in there. I spent many days reciting the Nembutsu[2] without lying down. Many, many days thus passed, with a mind full of vexations, without ever being able to find out what the Bright Virtue was.

"As the body was thus unsparingly and ruthlessly treated day and night, my buttocks grew sore and the skin was broken, which was very painful. But as I was quite strong those days I never laid myself down, even for

---

[1] Zazen means to sit cross-legged and meditate.
[2] *Nembutsu* is to repeat the Buddha's name, "*namu amida butsu, namu amida butsu*".

a day. I got several sheets of soft paper which were placed underneath my seat, as the bleeding from the broken parts troubled me. I had to change the soiled sheets frequently. I sometimes used cotton wadding instead of paper. With all this, I never allowed myself to rest in bed even for a day or for a night. I struggled hard like this for several years, and the outcome was that one day I was taken suddenly ill. I became a sick man, while the problem of the Bright Virtue remained unsolved. Yet I had indeed exercised myself most strenuously, but so far unsuccessfully.

"My disease grew gradually worse and worse, and I felt weaker and weaker. When I spat, the phlegm was found mixed with blood about the size of the thumb-head, which later turned into globules of bloody sputum. I once expectorated against the wall and discovered that the bloody sputa rolled down in drops along the surface. The kindhearted people were worried over my condition and persuaded me to nurse myself quietly in the retreat. I was given a servant, who would look after me.

"The illness at last evidently reached a critical stage. I could not take anything solid except rice-milk, and I made up my mind that I was going to die. Although I had no special attachment to this world, I greatly regretted passing away without resolving the great problem of life. While I was thus deeply absorbed in thought I felt some irritation in my throat which made me spit. What came out was a black mass of phlegm which rolled in drops, and this somehow eased my chest, when all of a sudden the idea flashed through the mind that all things in the world are readily dealt with by the thought of the Unborn. With this thought occupying the whole field of consciousness, I realized that I had been on the wrong track all the time, and had wasted a great deal of my energy for nothing.

"I now felt altogether rejuvenated and was happy beyond description. The desire for food returned, and I at once asked the nurse-servant to prepare rice gruel for me. He was wonder-struck because the sick man on the verge of death, unable until now even to sip rice-milk, demanded something more substantial. But greatly pleased with the order he hastened to prepare the gruel. He was in such a hurry to make it, and I was so impatient to have it even before it was fully done, that the gruel still contained some grains of rice not completely cooked. I quickly finished two or three bowls of it, but it did not hurt me. Gradually becoming better and better, I am still alive.[1]

"Having achieved what I desired, I talked to mother all about it, and when she died she was a happy person. And since I had this experience, I never came across any-one who could refute me. But if I had had someone when I was frantically seeking my way out who could have told me how to proceed I should not have so unneces-sarily exercised myself in search of the truth. The long years of my arduous quest have weakened the body a great deal, and I am not now a strong man. This grieves me because I am not able to come out to meet you as much as I should like, and talk to you about the Unborn.

"In those days I experienced a great deal of difficulty in finding a proper person who could testify to my dis-covery of the Unborn. There was one, it is true, who came from China and was staying in the city of Nagasaki. He was all very well as far as he went. In fact the rarity of good masters was a disconcerting matter. The reason I came out daily to meet you was to bear witness to your satori when you had one. You are to be congratulated on your access nowadays, for I am always ready to testify to your experience. If you have an experience, don't be afraid of coming to speak to me. If not, listen to my talk and decide for yourselves."

[1] Bankei must have been at least seventy when this was delivered at Aboshi, his native town.

VII

What then is this Unborn? Let Bankei speak for himself: "What every one of you has got from your parents is no other than the Buddha-mind, and this mind has never been born and is full of wisdom and illumination. As it is never born, it never dies. But I don't call it the Never-dying (immortal). The Buddha-mind is unborn, and by this unborn Buddha-mind all things are perfectly well managed.

"All the Buddhas of the past, future, and present, and all the Patriarchs who have successively appeared among us, are nothing but names given to individuals after their birth, and, therefore, from the point of view of the Unborn, they are, every one of them, secondary, derivative, and not of the Essence itself.

"When you are abiding in the Unborn you are abiding in the Source itself where all the Buddhas and Patriarchs come from. When you are convinced in thought that the Buddha-mind is the Unborn, nobody can detect where you are; even Buddhas and Patriarchs are unable to locate you, you are entirely unknown to them. When you have come to this decisive conviction, it is enough for you to sit quietly on the *tatami*[1] and be a living *Nyorai* (Tathagata), and it is not necessary to exercise yourself as arduously as I did.

"From the very moment you come to this decisive conviction you have an eye opened to see people properly. This is my own experience. Since I have gained the eye of the Unborn I have never once judged people wrongly. The eye is the same with everybody. Hence our school is known as the Clear-eyed. Again, when you come to this decisive conviction you are in the unborn Buddha-mind, you live in it, with it; the Buddha-mind is what you have from your parents. Hence another name for our school is the Buddha-mind school. . . .

---

[1] The straw mats which form the floor in a Japanese house.

"Once you come to this conviction that the Buddha-mind is unborn and illuminating, you will never be deceived by others. The entire world may claim that the raven (black) is the crane (white), but when you know through your everyday experience that by nature the raven is black and the crane is white, you can never be deceived. In the same way, when you come to this decisive conviction that the Buddha-mind is unborn and illuminating, and that with this unborn Buddha-mind one can manage all things, you will never be brought to believe wrongly, never be put in a false position, never be led astray. Such are the persons of the Unborn, living Tathagatas, to the end of the world. . . ."

From this account of Bankei's realization, we can see what kind of approach he had to Zen, and how arduously and self-sacrificingly he applied himself in search of an unknown treasure in a realm filled with unknowabilities, and finally what was the outcome of his adventure of so many years. While we have yet to know in detail more about the thoughts which occupied his mind during his austere life, we can to some extent outline the course he had to go through until he attained his satori, and this outlining will also help us to understand generally what is satori, so prized by the Zen masters.

Bankei started with the Bright Virtue which is the central problem in the teaching of the *Great Learning*. Most Confucians take it for granted that there is such a thing as the Bright Virtue, and their business, they consider, is simply to follow the formulated course of instruction given by their teachers. They generally look outward for certain prescribed rules. It was different with Bankei; he wished to see what the so-called Bright Virtue was, with his own eyes, and to take hold of it with his own hands. A mere generalization never satisfied him. He wanted to grapple with a concrete thing, and this is where Zen is the strongest; indeed it is the very thing that distinguishes Zen from all other teachings, religious or philosophical. Bankei had to come to Zen.

To know means to set the object of knowledge against

the knower. Knowledge always implies a dichotomy, and for this reason it can never be the thing itself. We know something about it, that is, the knowable part of it, which of course is not the whole thing. As far as knowledge is concerned, it stands outside the thing, can never enter into it, but to know the thing really in the true sense of the term means to become the thing itself, to be identified with it in its totality, inwardly as well as outwardly.

But how can one identify oneself with the object one wishes to know? To know is to stand outside, and if this does not give one true knowledge of it, one has to be merged in it, suppressing oneself altogether. But when this takes place the knower is no more there, he is lost, and with him merged in the object knowledge itself becomes impossible. To know, then, means not to know. Knowledge is ignorance, and ignorance is knowledge. We cannot, however, rest with this contradiction; there must be some way to transcend knowledge and yet to uphold it.

When I am I am, and when I say this I seem to know what this "I" is. But in reality I do not know it; my knowledge of it is not its whole, not itself but something objectified and alien to me as the knower. It stands outside me or facing me. The "I" of "I am" is not the "I" of "I know". There is a separation of "I", and this separation is the cause of all my spiritual vexations. The existing "I", that is, the living "I" is no more here; it is dissected and murdered. Being thus murdered "I" groans. Bankei exhausted himself and almost died to be released of these groans, and the "I" came to itself only when he had satori.

Satori may be regarded in one sense as a sort of knowledge, because it gives information regarding something. But there is a qualitative difference between satori and knowledge; they are essentially incommensurable. Knowledge gives only a partial idea of the thing known and this from an external point of view, whereas satori is the knowledge of the whole thing, of the thing in its totality, not as an aggregate of parts, but as something indivisible, complete in itself. And in satori this un-differentiated totality is comprehended from inside, so to speak. The totality, however, comprehended in satori has in fact no inside, no outside, as it transcends all such differentiations. Satori is thus seen to be, from the epistemological point of view, something unique in the field of knowledge.

Faith may be said to resemble satori in this, that it is an absolute correspondence between its object and the individual's entire subjectivity or personality or being. But as long as God is conceived to be existing externally as an object of faith, the faith is not satori. In satori God is subject, not object; God is in the individual, occupies the whole field of his being, and the individual is in God, of God, and completely united to him. In satori God becomes conscious of himself; until then he was in no relationship with me; with satori he begins to do his work, to be himself; he makes himself known to me. God is myself and yet not quite myself. God and I are not one and the same being; they are two, yet one; they are one, yet two. Satori is, therefore, to be won with my whole personality, and not with a divided self, not with a part of my personality, i.e. not by means of intellection.

In satori as well as in faith there is no question of abstraction, of generalization, of universality. When we say that satori is an experience, it is not quite correct, for it is what makes all our experiences possible and not one single experience to be differentiated from others. It transcends experience in its ordinary sense, yet it is in every experience. When we talk about an experience, it is something happening to one's individuality, is something externally added to it and affecting it to make a response in a certain specific manner. But in satori no such external and partial effect takes place in the field of consciousness.

Psychologically speaking, the satori-experience is a spontaneous self-stirring-up of the unconscious as constituting the foundation of one's personality, and not as something submerged in the consciousness as is commonly supposed. The unconscious, waking up to itself in satori, is a kind of cosmic unconsciousness, and all our individual consciousnesses are constructed with it as basic framework. It is here that satori gains its ontological significance, going beyond a mere psychological event.

While Bankei was trying to apprehend the Bright Virtue as something to be experienced with a part of his personality, that is, objectively, as the object of his intellectual self, he could not succeed; the more arduous his pursuit, the further receded the object from him; it was like running after his own shadow, and the result was utter exhaustion and the collapse of his whole being. Such a pursuit meant the continuous cutting-up of the whole cloth. It was inevitable that Bankei should present a pitiable sight. But the strange thing is that truth reveals itself only after the superficial structure of one's being gives way.

It was significant that Bankei started with the Confucian Bright Virtue and ended with the discovery of the Unborn, which is a Buddhist idea. The Confucian teaching is threaded through by ethical concepts, which is in conformity with the Chinese pragmatic mentality. The Chinese mind is not very strong in philosophy and China had no great philosophers until Indian thought infiltrated into it through the mediumship of Buddhism. Without the Buddhist stimulation China might have stayed solidly Confucian with no religions, with no metaphysics worth mentioning.

While Bankei's religio-philosophical consciousness was first aroused by the Bright Virtue, he could not go on with it long if he really wanted, as he did, to sound the very depths of his own being. He went around among the Buddhist teachers and with them he read the sutras, recited the Nembutsu, and practised the mystic rites after the Shingon school. They were all right so far as they went, but evidently none of them satisfied him, and he decided to follow the course prescribed by Zen, that is, to practise Zazen. He must have found something in it which was congenial to his temperament or predisposition. When he had satori, and after a further meditation upon it, he decided that the idea of the Unborn was the best expression for his satori and also the most fitting instrument to awaken the people of his day to the realization of satori.

The Unborn was the content of Bankei's satori which sprang up from his whole being, and enveloped it, so that he felt as if he were living in and with the Unborn all the time. Every moment of his life was the expression of the Unborn. The Unborn with him, therefore, was not a static conception; he did not intuit it spatially but temporally; he lived it, and while living he knew that he was it—which is satori.

Bankei identifies the Unborn with the Buddha-mind, and says that every sentient being is endowed with this mind. By it we sense, feel, reason, imagine, and carry on our human affairs. Hence the Unborn is bright and illuminating. These belong to the old vocabulary, and what Bankei means is that the Unborn is not an empty abstraction or a conceptual generalization, but a living, vital, concrete, individual idea.

Satori, therefore, absolutely belongs to the one who has it; it is neither communicable nor transferable nor subject to partition. It is itself, its own authority, its own witness, and does not require, strictly speaking, anybody's confirmation. It is sufficient unto itself. No amount of sceptical argument can refute it, because scepticism itself has to assume it, that is to say, it takes for granted the existence of the sceptic himself. He cannot, with all the cunning of his ratiocination, refute his individual identity. The sceptic succeeds only when he has a satori himself; but in this case he is denying his own scepticism; in other words he is upholding satori.

Naturally, those who have satori speak with authority and would not yield their ground to any objectors or sceptics. They declare that "since I have understood the one-finger Zen of Tenryu my whole life is not enough to be made full use of it", or "Whoever may appear, Buddhas or Patriarchs, before me and deny my satori—they will most assuredly get my thirty blows."

When Bankei was preaching at Sanyu-ji in the province of Bizen he was visited by a learned Buddhist priest of the Nichiren sect. This priest was noted for his scholarship, but did not like Bankei, partly for his popularity, which overshadowed his own. The priest was looking for a chance to clinch an argument with him. In the middle of Bankei's discourse, the priest said loudly, "I do not believe a word of yours. How can you save a person like myself?" Bankei beckoned him to come forward, and the priest at once responded. But Bankei wanted him to come nearer, and said, "Please come a little nearer yet." The priest made a forward movement again, when Bankei remarked, "How well you understand me!"

If the priest-scholar wanted to succeed in refuting Bankei, he had to succeed in refuting his own existence. If this were impossible, no one could overturn Bankei's position.

To make this idea of the Unborn more intelligible to the general audience, he used to give them the following: "When you were coming this way to hear my sermon, or when you are actually listening to it, suppose you hear a bell or a crow. You at once recognize that the bell is ringing or the crow is crying, and you do not make any mistake. It is the same with your seeing; you pay no special attention to a certain thing, but when you see it you at once know what is what. It is the Unborn in you that works these miracles, and as long as you are all like that, you cannot deny the Unborn, which is the Buddha-mind, bright and illuminating."

This argument may seem to suggest the unconscious or instinct, and not necessarily Bankei's conception of the Unborn, which is in truth far deeper and of a more spiritual significance. In point of fact, Bankei has been very much misunderstood in this respect. It need not be specially mentioned that the Unborn is brought into actuality by means of the instinctive or unconscious reaction to sense-stimuli and their psychological complications; but the main point is that all these conscious and unconscious activities on the part of each individual are gathered up by the basic notion of "I am" or "I exist". Descartes' dictum, "*Cogito ergo sum*",[1] will be, according to Bankei, "*Sento* (or *percipio*) *ergo sum*",[2] and when this "*sum*" is apprehended in its deepest sense we have the Unborn.

Those who stop at the psychological interpretation of the unconscious reactions will never be able to understand Bankei. They may elaborate on the notion of self-consciousness, but this will never bring them to the Unborn, because this intellectual elaboration is nothing but a murderous attempt to dissect the "I am" on the table of ratiocination. The "I am" must preserve its totality and viability if we are to come to the idea of the Unborn. Descartes' "*sum*" is epistemological and therefore dualistic, and has not yet touched the rock-bed of existence, the very foundation of the world, the source of all things. Descartes is the philosopher and Bankei the Zen master. What distinguishes the one from the other is perhaps, also, what we observe between the Western and the Eastern mind.

From these discussions we can see how natural and inevitable it was for Bankei to put all he had, or rather all he was, into the business of reaching the Unborn. Christ teaches (Matt. vii, 7), "Ask, and it shall be given you; seek and ye shall find; knock, and it shall be opened unto you." We may think this asking, seeking, and knocking is the simplest possible thing to do, but in reality it is no easy thing; indeed there will be no response from God unless this "simple" deed is done with our whole existence; that is, unless we die to ourselves, we can never be born again. Hence the symbolism of resurrection. One of the noted modern Zen masters in Japan, Bunan (1603–76), says:

> While living, be a dead man, thoroughly dead;
> Whatever you do, then, as you will, is always good.

---

[1] I think, therefore I am.
[2] I feel (or perceive), therefore I am.

To be living and yet to be dead, or to be dead and yet to be living, is, as far as our logic goes, an impossibility; but this impossibility is asked by the Zen master to be put in practice; and it is said that when this is practised all our deeds are appraised good. But it is good to remember that before this impossibility becomes practicable one has to go through all the experiences suffered by Bankei and other Zen masters. That the door opens to our knocking is no easy task; our whole existence must first be thrown down at the door.

Satori is "an existential leap" which means also an existential leaping-back. In our spiritual life there is no "one way" passage; the movement is always circular, the going-out is the going-in, and *vice-versa*. Bunan's dead-living man is Bankei's Unborn.

However varied these approaches to Zen, they are all characterized by the desire to grasp something which is beyond the realm of knowledge as popularly understood. This means that the aspirants for Zen are never satisfied with definitions or interpretations or postulations; they want something really concrete, personal, individualistic, something they can claim to be their own, something which gives them an inner satisfaction, something not added from outside but growing from within, something which they will never forget to carry along, as it always moves with them, following them like their own shadows, which they can never shake off even if so desired. This cannot, then, be anything else than their own Self.

The approach may be philosophical, emotional, religious, or practical, but their final objective is satori— the term given to Zen-experience or Zen-consciousness. Now satori has as already set out two aspects: psychological and metaphysical or epistemological. In the koan-exercise, the psychological aspect frequently comes up, strongly ignoring the metaphysical. But as long as satori is a certain definite view of life and the world, it may, for general readers, be better expressed in terms of philosophy, with the reservation, however, that Zen is something unique and expresses itself best in its own phraseology which, when translated into any other form, not only loses its vitality but ceases to be itself.

When satori is viewed in this way, we find that it is not confined to Zen, for it is found among followers of the Pure Land school, and in some sense in a more genuine form because of their not being hampered by the koan exercise. The Pure Land devotees are not intellectually inclined, as are Zen people. They aspire for a life in the Pure Land which is governed by Amida, and it is only there that they can attain full enlightenment. While they are here on earth, all that they can realize is the conviction that they are in a most definite manner destined for it and not for hell where, if they were left to themselves, they are sure to fall. Although the conviction or assurance they may have while here that they will be reborn in the Pure Land is to all intents and purposes the same as their already being there in the presence of Amida, the Jodo (Pure Land) teaching, as far as it is popularly interpreted, emphasizes a life after death in the Pure Land.

Whatever this be, their being assured of the rebirth is their satori; at least this is the way Zen followers would like to interpret the rebirth-assurance. They would equate the Nembutsu with the koan and often compare the efficacy of each method as an aid to the realization of satori. The Nembutsu in its strict sense is not a koan, though it has its own history and is meant to work in its own way. They are not to be confused.

Hakuin, the greatest devotee of the koan-system in modern Japan, gives an account of two Pure Land followers who gained satori by means of Nembutsu. They were known as Yenjo and Yengu. They were devoted to saying the Nembutsu, and Yenjo first reached the stage of self-identification when he came abruptly to a realization, being definitely convinced of his rebirth in the Pure Land. He started from Yamashiro, where they had their residence, to Yenshu to see a master called Dokutan Rojin.

Tan asked: "Where do you come from?"

Yenjo answered: "From Yamashiro."

Dokutan: "What is the school you belong to?"

Yenjo: "The Pure Land school."

Dokutan: "What is the age of Amida Nyorai?"

Yenjo: "He is of the same age as myself."

Dokutan: "What is yours?"

Yenjo: "Same as Amida's."

Dokutan: "Where is he this very moment?"

Yenjo clenched his left hand and raised it a little. Dokutan was surprised to find what kind of rebirth-assurance this Jodo devotee could have attained by means of the Nembutsu. The other one, Yengu, is also said before long to have attained the assurance.

With the Shin-shu followers, the Nembutsu is not so emphasized as in the Jodo, of which the Shin is a branch. They both hold firmly to the rebirth idea. The Shin teaches that the rebirth is the deed of "one thought" (*ichinen*), and therefore that you are assured of it by saying the Nembutsu, *namu amida butsu*, just once and no more. You do not have to wait until your death to be assured of the rebirth; the assurance comes to you while you are still living here on earth. It is an accomplished fact in your daily life, which is technically known as *Heizei-gojo* (literally, "daily-life deed-done"). How can this be attained? How can one Nembutsu accomplish this? How does the other-power of Amida work out this miracle? How can we be assured of it?

Monodane Kichibei (1803–1880), one of the most representative modern Shin devotees, attained the rebirth-assurance by resolutely grappling with the problem of death. He was intensely troubled with the idea of death, as it approaches us every minute sparing any of us, no matter how wise or stupid we may be. He read of *Heizei-gojo*, the assurance attained in one's lifetime, and wanted to know if this was really the case, and if so wanted to find a person who had actually experienced it and to receive instruction, if possible, from him. When he thought of these things he could not sleep; he did not

know what to do with himself. He talked the matter over
with his wife and asked her leave to let him go away for
some time in search of a good teacher.

He went from one teacher to another as recom-
mended and asked if they could die in peace before
they were fully assured of the rebirth. Nobody could
give him a satisfactory answer. He wandered from one
province to another without realizing how far away he
was from his home. Nor was he conscious of the time that
elapsed since he left his family. When he came back
without attaining his objective he was surprised to find
his baby grown so big that he did not recognize it.

In the meantime he heard of a good priest in his
neighbourhood, and hastened to visit him. He stayed
with him for some time, asking him all kinds of questions
regarding the Shin teaching. But finally he found the
priest was not the person he wanted. He went to Osaka
and called on the priest of the Saihoji. After questioning
the priest on all points that had been troubling him, he
finally said, "Pressed like this, I cannot die."

The Saihoji priest then asked, "Is it all right if you can
die?" So saying, he took out the *Ryoge-mon*[1] and made
Kichibei answer as to his understanding of the text. While
going through this examination, Kichibei opened his eye,
fully recognizing the Saihoji as the person who could
really help him in his search of "the other-power".

The Sayings of Kichibei, from which I have quoted the
above, does not specifically refer to the fact of his rebirth-
assurance, but the Saihoji priest evidently made him take
off one by one the heavy layers of the self-power idea
under which Kichibei had been groaning for so long. To
do this, the Saihoji used the *Ryoge-mon* as a scalpel,

[1] The *Ryoge-mon* or *Gaige-mon* is a short tract containing less than 100
words. *Ryo-ge* means "understanding", and *gaige* "repentance", and *mon* is
"tract" or "text". It tells that an absolute assurance of rebirth in the Pure
Land is gained on embracing unconditionally and wholeheartedly the
idea of other-power, giving up everything relating to self-power, such as
moral ideas and disciplinary measures. For as long as there is the slightest
trace of self, there will be no assurance of Amida's helping hands over you;
as long as your mind cherishes even an infinitesimal amount of egoism, there
will be no room for Amida to fix his abode there.

and Kichibei was made to shed the last trace of self-power which was so tenaciously clinging to him. For the text teaches an absolute other-power doctrine, rejecting even the desire to hear—as issuing from self-power—the desire which is ordinarily legitimate enough on the part of the devotee who wants to be assured of a rebirth while living this life of relativity.

The Saihoji was quite positive on this point and asked Kichibei: "Are you not still cherishing the thought of 'I have heard it'? Again, are you thoroughly free from the thought 'I was made to hear it'?" To this Kichibei answered, "I cannot express myself as having heard it, nor can I say that I have not heard it." The Saihoji said, "It is just as you say, Kichibei-san; nothing exceeds the importance of understanding Buddhism."

In spite of a superficial calmness, there is in Shin as much turbulent current and dialectical subtlety as in Zen. Shin does not swing a stick or staff, does not resort to ejaculations, but there are genuine seekers of truth and salvation in Shin as in Zen, and the clearness of vision, the security of the ground they tread, the exercise of an expansive, compassionate community-feeling conspicuously met with among Shin devotees. And the significant fact is that the real living force of Shin resides among its lay-devotees and not among the professional priesthood.

The Shin does not flaunt satori as Zen does, but there is no doubt that it exists also in Shin. Shin, however, has none of the psychology which comes out prominently in Zen, especially in connection with the koan exercise. Shin emphasizes the hearing instead of the seeing; the hearing is more passive, while the seeing is more mobile, active, and intellectual. As it teaches other-power, Shin naturally rejects activities of the self in any pattern. There are no dialectics in it; it does not say, "Hear, and yet do not hear", or "It is the bridge and not the river that flows"; it simply tells us to hear, hear, all the time, and does not demand of us to give out its sequence.

The Shin followers have no expectation of satori as

the koan followers; they simply want "to understand" what they hear, so as to make it develop into an assurance of rebirth while yet here, which is *Heizei gojo*. As long as there is a trace of self-consciousness as to hearing, or being made to hear, or somebody hearing, there is no real hearing, hence no assurance. Unless there is a kind of satori in Shin, there cannot be any such hearing, for this is not within the reach of reasoning or postulation. Says Kichibei, "When all the idea of self-power based upon moral values and disciplinary measures is purged, there is nothing left in you that will declare itself to be the hearer, and just because of this you do not miss anything you hear (in regard to the Shin teaching)."

The *Sayings of Kichibei* is full of such deeply religious pronouncements, and there are many Shin devotees who can genuinely appreciate them and, more than that, are actually living them. The fact is undeniable that there are more genuine and practically-working cases of satori among lay-devotees of Shin than in the equivalent Zen circles. This is principally due, I think, to the absence in Shin of the koan methodology. Shin devotees are not generally so learned or intellectually-inclined, and therefore not so vociferous; they silently work out their assurance in daily life. They feel so blessed and cheerful and thankful for Amida's merciful watch over them, and they feel this especially when they are gathered about the leader who devotes himself unselfishly, ungrudgingly to the cause.

Some of such devotees are quite illiterate, but the spiritual truths they express are wonderful. Here are some of them: the author known as Saichi was born in the province of Iwami, and died recently at the age of eighty-three. He was originally a carpenter but his last business was as maker of and dealer in footwear of the Japanese style. His education was limited, and the poems he composed while working on the *geta* (wooden sandals or clogs) and written on the shavings are mostly in the *kana* style of writing and not very correct either. The translations are free:

The world is folly, I am folly, Amida is folly;
Whatever they may be, they are saved by the parental
    folly.
Namu-amida-butsu.

This I with an eye given by thee,
The eye that sees thee.
Namu-amida-butsu.

Where are you, Saichi? In the Pure Land?
This the Pure Land:
Namu-amida-butsu.

Hearing the name of Amida the Buddha.
This the Buddha becoming Saichi,
This Buddha no other than namu-amida-butsu.

Adopted, the mind,
The first visit to the Pure Land;
And back again among the defilements of this world,
Commissioned to help all beings.

V

THE KOAN

I

THERE are three problems demanding solution which confront every sincere Buddhist. While they are unsolved he cannot have any peace of mind. What are the three? 1. Who or what is the Buddha? 2. What is the Mind? 3. Whence do we come and whither do we go?

The first question, "What is the Buddha?" is an inquiry regarding the nature of Enlightenment (*bodhi*, *satori*). A Buddha means "an enlightened one". To ask "What is Buddha?" is the same as asking what enlightenment is. When we attain enlightenment we are Buddhas, that is to say, we are all in possession of the Buddha-nature. The only difference between the Buddha and ourselves is that we are not yet enlightened, as we keep the Buddha-nature enveloped in defilements (*klesha*, *bonno*).

To become a Buddha, therefore, it is necessary to wipe off the defilements on our Buddha-nature. This makes us face a second question, "What are the defilements?" If we share the Buddha-nature with the Buddha, cannot we all be Buddhas from the first? Where can the defilements come from which veil the Nature and keep us from being Buddhas? This brings us to the second great problem, "What is the Mind?"

In most Buddhist texts the mind (*hsin* in Chinese and *kokoro* in Japanese) is used in a double sense. The one is "mind", in the sense of human consciousness, while the other is a kind of universal mind, an over-soul, the highest principle from which the universe with all its manifoldness starts. When Buddhists ask what the mind is, they mean the latter kind of mind, and identify it with the Buddha-nature. The two terms, Mind (*hsin*) and Nature (*hsing*) are interchangeable. When we know the one we know the other. When a man attains Buddhahood he sees the Mind. The Mind is what makes up Buddhahood. The Buddha-nature is the Mind and the Mind is the Buddha-nature. The first problem is, therefore, reducible to the second, and the second to the first.

The problem of birth-and-death (*samsara*)[1] is also finally that of the Mind as well as that of the Nature. When you know the Nature or the Mind you know whence you are born and whither you pass, and this knowledge releases you from the bondage of birth-and-death. You become free or, rather, you realize that you have from the very beginning of things been absolutely free. This realization of freedom is attaining Buddhahood and seeing into the Mind. All the three problems which harass every serious-minded Buddhist are interrelated; when the one is picked up the other two come along with it; the untying of one knot means at once the untying of all three.

According to where the emphasis is placed, we talk of the Buddhist discipline as aiming at delivery from birth-and-death, or at attaining Buddhahood or enlightenment, or at seeing into the Mind. The Zen motto, "It directly points to the Mind; it makes us see into the Nature, and Buddhahood is attained," shows the relationship between Mind and Buddha-nature.

The problem of birth-and-death shows a somewhat different aspect of the one fundamental problem, for while the Mind or the Nature points to the basis of reality, birth-and-death is concerned with the phenomenal side of it. If the Mind or the Nature is something above birth-and-death, that is, if it transcends all forms of

[1] Birth-and-death is a technical term in Buddhism and is better hyphenated. The Sanskrit original *samsara* means "becoming" or "passing through a succession of changes", for which the Chinese Buddhist scholars have "birth-and-death". It stands contrasted to Nirvana which is "changelessness", "eternity", "absoluteness". To transcend birth-and-death is to be released from the bondage of *karma*, to attain emancipation, enlightenment and eternal bliss, which is Buddhahood.

mortality and transiency, how can there be this world which is essentially contrary to the notion of the Mind or the Nature? The question is similar to, in truth the same as the one which Christian theologians encounter: "How could God—all perfect and good in every way—create a world full of evil and imperfections?"

Buddhists always contrast the Buddha-nature with birth-and-death, and urge us to return to the Nature. But if we are all endowed with the Nature which is the opposite of birth-and-death, how have we come to this world of impermanence, there to go through all kinds of suffering? This is an eternal contradiction, and is inherent in our nature. As long as we are what we are there is no escape from it, and this fact is really what drives us all, sooner or later, into the fold of spiritual discipline.

This contradiction, or the rising above it, is known among Zen followers as "This Matter", "This Way", or "This One Great Event". To become aware of the contradiction means to transcend it, and this transcending constitutes "The Matter". For Zen the transcending is the awareness, which makes up the content of the Zen experience. This experiencing is clearing up "This Matter", or simply "The Matter", or "The Event", or, to use the Confucian term, "The Way". Here all forms of logical contradiction are dissolved, because "The Matter" is the point where this dissolution takes place. Herein Zen attains its end.

According to Daiye (1089–1163), of the Sung Dynasty, the Zen follower stands against the following problems: "Whence are we born? Whither do we go? He who knows this whence and whither is the one to be truly called a Buddhist. But who is this one who goes through birth-and-death? Again, who is the one who knows not anything of the whence and whither of life? Who is the one who suddenly becomes aware of the whence and whither of life? Who is the one, again, who, facing this koan, cannot keep his eyes fixed, and as he is not able to comprehend it, feels his internals put out of order as if a fiery ball, swallowed down, could not readily be ejected?

"If you wish to know who this one is, apprehend him where he cannot be brought within the fold of reason. When you thus apprehend him, you will know that he is, after all, above the interference of birth-and-death."

In this we see that Daiye puts the entire emphasis of his discourse on the problem of birth-and-death, and what is most significant with him is his reference to the one who is conscious of himself over the whole area of his activities in such a way that this "consciousness" cannot be brought into our ordinary relatively-limited field of consciousness. For when you try to catch him in this way he always eludes us; when you think you have finally caught him, what is left in your hands is nothing but an empty shadow of him, an abstract concept which gives you no actual help in your everyday life. It is where you play with all your dialectical subtleties.

Zen is never satisfied with such intellectual chimeras; Zen wants to take hold of the one who breathes through every fibre of your tissue and vibrates with every beat of your pulse. This is what might be called super-consciousness or unconscious consciousness. In regular Buddhist terminology, it is undiscriminated discrimination, the mind of mindlessness, or unthought thought. But these still sound too empty for the Zen stomach to digest, and the masters have their own way of expressing "This Matter":

"When I was in Ching-chou district, I had *pu chen* (a simple dress) made which weighed seven *chin*."

"1, 2, 3, 4, 5, 6, 7; 7, 6, 5, 4, 3, 2, 1. The Yellow River bending its course nine times flows from the Kun-lung Mountains. Mahaprajna-paramita."

"The spring mountains are seen piling up one layer of
    green over another;
The spring streams are reflecting, as they flow away,
    shadows of green.
A figure, solitariness itself, between Heaven and Earth
Stands, alone, before an infinitely expanding vista."

I have been digressing. What I wish to state is this: From whatever direction you come to Zen, you encounter the one who is variously named as he manifests himself in varieties of things. Daiye, in the quotation above cited, shows us the way through the gate of birth-and-death, leading us to the presence of the one who is unconsciously conscious of himself. In the following, Yakusan (751–834) directly attacks the problem of the Buddha-nature and the Mind, which demonstrates itself in negation as well as in affirmation, in death as well as in birth, which is seen where negation is affirmation and affirmation is negation, that is, where there is birth-and-death and also where there is neither birth nor death. This may sound confusion worse confounded, even absolute nonsense. But Zen, from the intellectual point of view, can be regarded as thriving on nonsense.

When Yakusan first came to Sekito (700–790) he asked: "As to the Three Pitaka and the Twelve Divisions of Buddhist Scripture, I have made some advance in their study; but as to the teaching prevailing now in the South, which point directly to our Mind whereby seeing into the Nature makes us attain Buddhahood, I have no knowledge whatever. May I ask your instruction in this?"

Said Sekito, "Affirmation avails not, nor does negation, nor does affirmation-negation." (This means: "To say 'it is' will not do; to say 'it is not' will not do; to say 'it is and is not' will not do, either.")

Yakusan failed to understand this, and Sekito advised him to go to Baso (–788) who was also engaged in teaching Zen in the West of the Yang-tze-Kiang. Yakusan came to Baso and asked the same question as the one proposed to Sekito. Baso replied:

"Sometimes I make him raise the eyebrows or twinkle the eyes; sometimes I make him not do that; it sometimes goes very well with him when he raises the eyebrows or twinkles the eyes; it sometimes goes very wrong with him when he does that."

This statement at once opened Sekito's eye to the

truth of Zen, but he did not know how to express himself; all that he could do was to bow to Baso with due respect. Remarked Baso, "Why this bowing, Yakusan?"

"When I was at Sekito's it was like a mosquito biting an iron bull." This was all Yakusan could say in way of response.

Before Yakusan became interested in Zen he was already a master of Buddhist philosophy, well versed in the teaching of the Tripitaka which covers the entire field of Buddhist thought and experience; but there was still something in his mind which could not be satisfied with mere abstractions and rationalistic arguments. When he heard of the Zen teaching, which deals with the Buddha-nature or Mind without any mediation, intellectual or otherwise, his spiritual curiosity was aroused. As far as dialectics were concerned he had enough of them, but he never expected to see the Buddhist truth presented in the fashion of the Zen masters, such as Sekito and Baso.

Sekito might be said to be on the track of dialectics, but Baso's statement in regard to the raising of the eyebrows and the twinkling of the eyes was quite extraordinary, and must have struck him to the quick. The innermost core of his heart, which had been sleeping, must have been violently touched.

Yakusan stayed with Baso for three years after this incident. One day Baso asked, "How are you getting on these days?" "Bared of the skin there stands one reality all by itself," was Yakusan's answer. Later he returned to his former teacher, Sekito. Sekito, finding him one day sitting cross-legged on the rock, asked, "What are you doing here?"

"Not one thing," replied Yakusan.

"If so, you are sitting idly."

"Even the sitting idly is doing something."

"You say, 'doing nothing', but pray what is that which is doing nothing?"

"Even when you call up thousands of wise men, they cannot tell you that."

Sekito heartily endorsed Yakusan's understanding of the truth of Zen.

Later, Sekito happened to make this remark to his congregation, "Neither words nor acts have anything to do (with Zen)." To this Yakusan added his comment, "Even things that are neither words nor acts have nothing to do (with Zen)." Sekito said, "Here in my place there is not a room even for the point of a needle to enter." Yakusan rejoined, "Here in my place it is like planting a flower on the rock." Both Sekito and Yakusan are talking about the same thing, however much they may seem disagreeing with each other. As long as they are talking about negations and contradictions, words and acts, they are on the plane of rationalism; it is only when they talk about the needle-point or the rock-flower that they are properly on the plane of Zen.

II

The third entrance to Zen is the problem of birth-and-death, which may be said to be the reverse side of that of the Buddha-nature or the Mind. The one in fact cannot be separated from the other. The Buddha-nature is regarded as pure and without defilement, but as long as it remains in itself it has no way of communicating itself to us; it is the same as non-existent. If we are to talk at all of the Nature or Mind, and wish to reach it, it must make itself in some way intelligible to us. It must at least show its tail-end whereby human consciousness can grasp it and expose the whole of it in the light.

The Buddha-nature is to be comprehended in and through birth-and-death, and birth-and-death must somehow harbour the Nature in it. The Nature is not to be taken hold of by running away from birth-and-death, that is, from the manifoldness of things. If the Nature is not in birth-and-death, it must be thought of as having its pure and undefiled residence outside the world, which is impure and defiled and encased in the passions (*klesha*). In this case there is a dualism of the Nature and birth-and-death, and the problem of evil, as is the case with Christian theology, will never yield to a solution, unless it is pushed aside as only concerning the will of God and altogether beyond the ken of the human understanding.

As has already been repeatedly shown, Zen is against dualism, as it holds the position which can never be attained through that approach. Even to make reference to this "position" is liable to be dualistically interpreted, for Zen's position may be designated as having no spatial-temporal references. To talk about birth-and-death is already committing oneself to certain limitations, and the Buddha-nature ceases to be pure and without defilement. Thus Zen teaches us to strike the path where purity and defilement, the Buddha-nature and birth-and-death, are self-identical.

The following mondo are, therefore, to be understood in the light thus gained:

A monk asked, "How can I get away from the triple[1] world?"

"Where are you now?" replied the master.

There was another monk who asked: "I wish to escape from this world of birth-and-death. What shall I do?"

"What is the use of escaping birth-and-death?" the master demanded.

"I wish to be given the regular Buddhist Precepts."

"What are you going to do with the Precepts?"

"I desire to be saved from the whirlpool of birth-and-death."

"There is the one who has nothing to do with birth-and-death and who has no use for the Precepts."

This is a subtler way of putting the problem of birth-and-death:

[1] Buddhism conceives this world of particulars as threefold: the world of form (*rupaloka*), the world of desire (*kamaloka*), the world of no-form (*arupaloka*).

"Anciently," a government official asked a master, "there was a man who kept a goose-chick in a bottle; after some time it grew bigger and the goose could not be got out of the bottle. The question now is: the bottle is not to be destroyed, nor is the goose to be hurt. O master, what means could there be to get the poor fowl out?"

The master, thus asked, called aloud, "O Governor!"

The governor responded, "Yes, master." Thereupon, the master triumphantly said, "There, the goose is out!"

Joshu was sweeping his garden when a monk entered and asked, "O master, you are a great enlightened master, and how is it that there is dust here to sweep?"

Joshu said, "It comes from outside."

Another monk once asked, "This is such a holy temple ground; how is it that there is dust to sweep?"

Joshu said, "Here comes another particle of dust."

Another monk asked, "What would you say when everything is thoroughly cleaned up and there is not a particle of dust?"

Said Joshu, "No vagabonds are permitted here."

In these mondo there are no obvious references to birth-and-death, but essentially they all revolve about this problem. What troubles us all is: "Why this birth-and-death when God himself is immortal and free from all traces of defilement? Why this eternal opposition between the Buddha-nature and beings enveloped in the passions or defilements (*klesha*)? Why this harassing struggle between pride and humility, between individualistic self-assertion and the giving up of oneself to something higher? In terms of Buddhist thinking, birth-and-death is on the one side and the pure undefiled Mind is on the other, and the question is how to bridge them. Practically, Zen's problem is ultimately the same as that which is encountered by every other religion, but that in Zen's approach to its solution there is something altogether unique, no parallels of which are discoverable in the annals of religious thought.

The statements: "All the worlds filling the boundlessness of space are not kept apart one from another at this tip of the hair; the ten periods of time, past and present, are not detached, from beginning till end, from this present moment," may not be unintelligible to most of us, who have more or less been philosophically trained, but when such mondo as the following appear, even the Zen devotees may find them difficult to fathom.

When Ko, the shami,[1] came to the residence of Yakusan, the master, he happened to be caught by rain, and Yakusan remarked, "Ko, you are come."

Ko said, "Yes, master."

"You are very wet."

"Do not play on such a drum, master."

Ungan, one of Yakusan's chief disciples, who chanced to be there, said, "When there is no hide, what drum do you beat?"

Dogo, another disciple, said, "When there is no drum, what hide do you beat?"

Yakusan concluded, "We have today had a very fine musical party."

At dinner-time one day Yakusan himself beat the drum to announce it. Ko came in dancing with his bowl. Yakusan, seeing this, threw the mallet down and said, "What harmony is this?"

Ko said, "A secondary one."

"What is the primary?"

Ko scooped a bowlful of rice out of the rice-holder and left the room.

There is a noted koan known as "Tosotsu's[2] Threefold Frontier-gate" in which the Buddha-nature's relationship to birth-and-death is well defined: "Those who in the study of Zen go on a pilgrimage through the whole country are desirous only of seeing into the Nature; let me ask then; (1) where is your Nature at this moment? (2) If

---

[1] Shramana, one who has not yet been ordained to full priesthood.
[2] One of the noted Sung masters, died 1091.

you have a glimpse into your own Nature, how do you
transcend birth-and-death at the moment when your eye-
sight is no more reassuring? (3) When you have trans-
cended birth-and-death, you know your destination;
Where, then, is your Nature when the four elements are
dissolving?"

III

Approaches to Zen are not limited to these three;
indeed there are an infinite number of them. As there are
so many individual minds, there are correspondingly so
many individual ways. Each of us has his private way not
to be trodden by others, and each solves his own problem
in his own way. All that the Zen master can do for him is
to give him a direction, to walk which is his own business.
The essential thing in the study of Zen is to attain satori.
As long as you have no satori there is no Zen for you; you
may have an abundance of good understanding in regard
to all scriptural and philosophical teachings, but you are
not a Zen follower unless your mind is awakened to a
certain spiritual truth.

Of old there was a monk who, while reading the
Pundarika (*Lotus*) *Sutra*, came across the passage, "All
things (*dharma*) from the first have been eternally in a
perfect state of tranquillity." This stirred his doubt, and
he could not feel settled in his mind. Walking and standing, sitting and lying, he pondered the statement in a
most serious frame of mind, but all to no avail. One
evening, however, while the moon was shining he heard a
nightingale sing, which opened his eye to the significance
of the passage in the *Lotus Sutra*, and he composed this:

All things from the first
Have been eternally quiet.
With the coming of the Spring
All the flowers are out,
And I hear the nightingale sing on the willow branch.

This is evidently no more than an objective description of the spring season, and there is nothing in it suggesting even tentatively what took place in the mind of the monk except the allusion to the scriptural passage. But to those who have gone through the same experience as the monk the stanza is full of vital importance. And wherever this is felt there is Zen, by what approach this may have come.

This will remind us of Sotoba's poem on Mount Lu which has already been given. Let me quote here Hakuin's thirty-one syllable poem on the sound of a snowfall:

> How I would have them hear,
> In the woods of Shinoda,
> At an old temple,
> When the night is deepening,
> The sound of the snowfall!

He was then absorbed in deep meditation while staying at an old countryside temple. The snow was falling fast, the night was advancing, the silence reigned, when probably some of the branches heavily laden with snow suddenly shook the burden off, producing a dull thud—which woke Hakuin from the absorption. The poem does not tell anything that took place in his inner mind; it merely describes it in objective terms. As far as its literal meaning goes, we have no means of sounding the depths of Hakuin's satori. It can only be appreciated by those who have actually gone through the same experience. So sings the Chinese poet:

> Let *sake* be taken with friends who really understand you;
> Let songs be sung to a company who knows how to appreciate you.

Daito's thirty-one-syllable poem, however, savours somewhat of a satori paradox which is about the spiritual cattle-herding:

> If you see with the ears
> And hear with the eyes,
> No doubts you will ever cherish:
> How naturally falls
> The rain dripping from the eaves!

"Naturally" is *onodzukara* in Japanese. The original is a very expressive term. I am not sure whether "naturally" conveys all that is implied in the Japanese. Besides naturalness or spontaneousness, *onodzukara* means suchness, thing-as-it-is-ness, which is, from the Zen understanding, more than hearing by the ears or seeing by the eyes—which is indeed seeing by the ears and hearing by the eyes; and this really means transcending the world of sense and intellect, entering into the state of things prior to the differentiation of light and darkness, good and bad, God and his creation.

Onodzukara in Daito's thirty-one-syllable poem, therefore, is to be understood in its deepest spiritual sense and not in its merely "natural" sense. This transformation of "natural" into "spiritual", or the mutual fusion taking place between the different sense-functions, constitutes the content of satori, and this is where the objective descriptions given by Hakuin and others impart an altogether different inspiration to those whose minds are Zen-inspired.

According to the Zen understanding of Buddhism, Buddhism may be likened to a circle at the centre of which Zen posits itself, and from this centre Zen radiates its lines of communication to every point of the circumference. Zen is thus sensitive to any event that may take place in the outer world. At the slightest touch Zen rushes out to meet it like the spider at the centre of his well-known web. Stating this psychologically, anything that happens at the periphery of human consciousness sends its vibration down to the Zen centre of unconsciousness, and those who are at all sensitive and at the same time critically reflective develop what may be called the Zen sense, which will gradually and eventually make them turn towards the Zen centre of unconsciousness. They will then begin to grope, though naturally still in utter darkness, with a trembling heart to see whether there is really such a centre in them.

This was the case with Yakusan, as we have already seen, and with many others. They were not satisfied with mere abstractions, they longed for something concrete and vital; they were satiated with what could be gained from mere learning, which did not really have much to do with their inmost self; they felt something urging within themselves which made them go ahead until they finally reached the Zen centre of unconsciousness, and awakened it to a state of consciousness, which is not, however, that which we have in the ordinary sense of the term. And this is no more than satori itself. All the drive they had could not but culminate in satori.

Banzan, one of Baso's disciples, says that satori, which is the highest stage of Zen realization we can reach, is not something which can be handed over from one person to another; that is to say, it is absolutely personal, being one's creative experience which is not repeatable nor transmissible to others. According to Jimyo, a great master of the Sung Dynasty, whatever satori thousands of masters are said to have had is not what it ought to be; that is to say, a satori that is at all describable as satori is not satori, for it is not any particular experience to be singled out of thousands of experiences one may have; in this case, satori will be one of the events happening to human consciousness which are definable and individually distinguishable.

Now Daito of Daitokuji, Kyoto, comments on these statements of the old masters, "These old masters are like two *kuei* (demons) quarrelling over a cask filled with black lacquer solution."[1] I would say satori is where every wise man walks, that is to say, satori is no exclusive possession of one particular individual, it is shared by every one of us, wise and ignorant, noble and low, rich and poor; the Zen centre of unconsciousness is the point where all our

[1] A vain wrangle in words like the pot calling the kettle black.

peripheral experiences turn back as well as start out. The point, however, is not something determinable by postulation or conceptualization.

Banzan, Jimyo, and Daito may appear to be disagreeing among themselves in regard to their understanding of satori as passing even beyond the limits of human consciousness. But in reality they are talking about the same thing, which is describable in every possible way by those who have satori. In any event, when there is no satori there is no Zen. The two are inseparable, they are identical. Now the question is: How can satori be made available to any student aspiring for Zen experience? Cannot satori be made more accessible to us who are not so highly or richly gifted as the ancient masters and yet who are quite desirous of experiencing it?

The old masters found their own way through the darkness of the Unconscious guided by sheer will-power and a never-satiated desire for a definite method, if there could be such, which would lead us then step by step to the realization. Although satori itself is not something transmissible from one person to another, that is, teachable by some means, oral or written, every one of us is so made by nature as to be for ever yearning for something like satori in his spiritual pilgrimage. If so, it is only kind of the masters to open up a road which points in the direction of satori.

The koan system of Zen thus came to being, and is now used by most Zen followers. *Koan* literally means "a public document", by which the Zen master is supposed to test the depths of understanding attained by his disciples. But in practice it is given them at present as a sort of problem to be solved. If we come to a Zen master to study Zen, he will produce one hand before us and demand to hear its sound. No sound, of course, comes out of one hand, and as far as our so-called common-sense goes, there is no hearing of any sound here. But here is the "trick" of Zen. It is by this nonsensical proposition that Zen drives us into a quandary from which we are expected in due course to extricate ourselves. This extrication means satori.

The "one hand" koan is the invention of Hakuin, one of the great Zen masters of seventeenth century Japan. Prior to him the most popular koan was "Mu" or "Muji". It is still in use along with the "one hand". *Muji* means the "character *mu*" (*wu* in Chinese, meaning "nothing" or "non-entity" or "no-being"). It originates from Joshu (778–897) of the T'ang Dynasty. When he was asked whether the dog had the Buddha-nature, he replied, "Mu," meaning "No, it has none." Whatever inner meaning it might have had in the mind of Joshu, the "Mu" as koan has no special reference to its origin. It is simply "Mu" and nothing else.

The "Mu" as koan was probably first used by Goso Hoyen (–1104), of the Sung Dynasty. No doubt it was one of the koan, or *wato*,[1] which he adopted as the means of opening the eyes of his disciples to the truth of Zen, but later it came to be almost exclusively used as the first eye-opening koan.

Before the koan system was invented a monk wishing to study Zen came to the monastery and spent his time mostly in meditation, but was also employed on the farm, raising vegetables, gathering kindlings, etc. Many attended sermons, or rather pithy epigrammatic discourses given by the master, and often asked him questions

[1] *Wato* literally means "story-head", but "head" has no special sense here. A story is a mondo or an incident that takes place between master and disciple, or it is a question given out by a master. Some of the *wato* used by Zen masters during the Sung and later dynasties are:

1. "All things are reducible to the One, but to what will this One be reduced?" Joshu said, "When I was in Seishu (Tsing-chou), I had one cotton robe made which weighed seven *kin* (chin)."

2. "When there is not one thought stirring in one's mind, is this faulty?" Answered Ummon, "Shumisen (The Mount Sumeru)!"

3. When the monk Myo asked Yeno (–713) about the secret truth of Zen, Yeno said, "Where is your original face which you have even before your parents gave birth to you?"

4. When Joshu was asked about the signification of the First Patriarch's coming from the west of China, he said, "The cypress tree (*Pai-shu-tsu*) in the courtyard."

5. "When you are dead, cremated, and the ashes scattered, where are you?"

regarding whatever doubt they cherished about Zen. But it was possible that some of them failed to find their way to the proper understanding of Zen, and there must have been many who wasted their time in meditating on abstractions, or just sitting quietly, trying to keep all their thoughts out of the field of consciousness.

The koan was meant to keep both groups in the right track; those who were intellectually inclined were saved from losing themselves in an endless maze of speculation, while the others who took Zen for the mere emptying of contents of consciousness were held back from committing a sort of mental suicide.

In the study of Zen these two tendencies are to be scrupulously guarded against, abstract conceptualization and absorption in emptiness. The koan keeps the mind from following either one of these two courses, it sets the mind in the middle way, for the truth of Zen is not in rationalistic abstraction nor in mere quietistic tranquillization. When left to itself the human mind is sure to tip either way, left or right, up or down, and the Zen masters, in fact all well-informed and observant Buddhists, have been aware of this inherent defect in human consciousness. They have advised us to practise *Shamatha* along with *Vipashyana*, or *Vipashyana* along with *Shamatha*.

Shamatha is the cessation of thoughts which disturb the mind, whereas Vipashyana is the keeping of our intellectual eye open to a world of changes. Shamatha, while aiming at the realization of the oneness of all things where the Dharmakaya of all the Buddhas becomes identified with the body of all sentient beings (*sarvasattva*), is apt to lead the mind to a state of lethargy and indifference; and to counterbalance this it is necessary to have the mind stimulated in one way or another, that is, it is important for Zen students to keep their attention engaged with subjects belonging to a world of particulars.

For this reason, Ashvaghosha, the author of *The Awakening of Faith*, strongly advises the practise of Shamatha and Vipashyana simultaneously. He says: "Whether walking or staying still, whether sitting or lying, you are to practise Shamatha and Vipashyana side by side. That is to say, while you are meditating on the self-nature of all things, which has never been subject to birth-and-death, you are to meditate on the karmic causation of acts good or bad, on the retribution of pain and pleasure, which will never be lost, nor destroyed. While thus meditating on the karmic causation and retribution of good and bad, you also meditate on the Nature that is beyond comprehension.

"When Shamatha is practised, it cures the unen-lightened people's (*prithagjana*) attachment to worldly things and saves the two *yana*[1] from holding up a timid and cowardly outlook on life. When Vipashyana is practised it cures the two *yana* of not arousing a great compassionate heart and of committing themselves to narrow-mindedness, and keeps the ignorant from not cultivating roots of good. For these reasons, these two courses of discipline, Shamatha and Vipashyana, com-plement each other and are not to be kept in separation. When you are not in possession of both, you cannot expect to enter upon the path of enlightenment."

These two courses have been running through the entire history of Zen Buddhism, sometimes happily in harmonious parallel, sometimes the one more strongly emphasized than the other. At the time of Gunin (602–675) the two courses were represented by two schools; the one put more stress on the Dhyana or Shamatha aspect of Zen, while the other insisted upon the Prajna or Vipashyana as being more essential of Zen. The separa-tion came to a crisis under Yeno (–713), who is regarded by his followers as the Sixth Patriarch of Zen in China. The rival school led by Jinshu (–706) did not thrive very long after him.

I will not enter here into a detailed discussion about the merits and demerits of the two schools, except to say

[1] Three *yana* (vehicles) are distinguished in Buddhism: Arhat, Pratyeka-buddha, and Bodhisattva. Mahayana Buddhism, including Zen, is meant for Bodhisattvas. The first two *yana* are too timid to face the world, being advocates of escapism. In this respect they are egoists.

that the school of the Sixth Patriarch, whose line of succession is the one represented by Zen followers in Japan as well as in China, can really be said to harbour the spirit of Zen. There are reasons for this assessment, one of which is that the essence of Zen is Prajna and not Dhyana.

While Prajna is variously understood, it essentially consists in the synthetic grasping of Shamatha and Vipashyana, of contemplation and intellection. It is a quietistic meditation in the oneness of things and at the same time an intellectual discrimination raised to its utmost limits. The term Zen etymologically comes from Dhyana and scholars are apt to take Zen to mean practising Dhyana as it was practised by the Indians, that is, being absorbed in the Absolute, which is tantamount to entering into Nirvana, the cessation of all activities. But as Zen is actually and historically understood it is far from being such a practice in self-annihilation; it is the understanding of things not only from the aspect of manyness but from the aspect of absolute oneness; it is to take hold of the one as embodying itself in the multitudeness of things, and not as standing aloof from them.

Even when Zen is absorbed in Dhyana, or Shamatha, or in meditation, it never loses sight of a world of sense and intellect. Zen is not only thought but non-thought; it discriminates and at the same time holds in itself that which transcends discrimination. It acts, but acts in such a way as not to have any purpose. Zen's life is not teleologically defined; it is like the sun's rising in the East and setting in the West; it is like the plants flowering in spring and bearing fruits in autumn. It is we humans who take all these phenomena of Nature as having some definite design in relation to human destiny and welfare, but this homocentric interpretation of the world always ends in tragedy, if not in an utter confusion of thought.

Zen's world is at once purposeless and purposeful; it is purposeful as long as we conceive it in terms of space and time and causation, but it is utterly purposeless when it takes us to a world where there is neither thinker nor that which is thought, nor what is known as a thought. Some may say that there is no such world as far as human understanding is concerned, but Zen would say that there is such a world, that we are actually living in it and do not know it. In point of fact, Zen is not to be refuted by arguments; when it says things are so, the affirmation is final, and the only thing you can do is either to accept or reject it. This is in the very nature of Zen, that is, of Prajna.

As far as practice goes, however, Zen is not a single-handed upholder of Prajna; it also advocates Dhyana without which Prajna is apt to evaporate into abstract nothingness. These two, Dhyana and Prajna, are not to be separated as Zen can thus preserve its wholesome stability, as well as its intuitive clarity and fluidity. Of the two schools of Zen Buddhism, the Soto tends to uphold the Dhyana aspect of Zen while the Rinzai is partial to the Prajna.

IV

The koan system, which was invented to help Zen followers attain satori by the easier method, has also something in it whereby the Prajna ideal of Zen becomes definitely realizable. By this I mean that the oneness of things is realized more as immanent in them, that the subject who sees is no other than the object that is seen, that when I lift a finger the whole world is revealed in it, that the ego which we take for a separate entity is no other than the world reflecting itself. This we may call the meta-logical or super-logical or meta-physical phase of satori.

But there is another side which one may designate as the psychological phase of satori, though satori itself is neither psychological nor metaphysical. Before the koan came in vogue, the psychological aspect of satori was not very strongly in evidence, for the approach to satori was mainly metaphysical or intellectual. When Godo Hoyen (–1104), for instance, came to Zen, he was compelled to do so by his intellectual doubt as to who it was that was conscious of all sense-experiences. When Butsugen (–1120) read the *Pundarika* (Lotus) *Sutra*, what puzzled him was the statement regarding the truth which is beyond the comprehension of the discursive understanding, and this made him come to Zen. When Bukkwa (–1135) became critically ill while young, he found that all his previously accumulated learning could not show him the way to Nirvana, which is beyond the limits of birth-and-death, whereby he decided to take up the study of Zen. Rinzai (–867), Reijun (845–919), Keichin (867–928) and others were strict observers of the Vinaya Precepts, but were never satisfied with being merely moral, blindly following rules of conduct which were set up by others, however exalted beings they had been. They desired to dig down deeply into the fundamentals of the so-called moral life; and this made them come to Zen.

This may be said to be the ethical approach to Zen, but what really made them abandon the idea of being merely eudemonistic was their intellectual urge. They must have applied themselves very hard indeed to the study of Zen, devoting many years to meditation, strenuous thinking and anxious inquiries; but as they did not have any special koan to grapple with, their course of study is not so marked psychologically as is the case with the koan devotee. What I mean by "psychologically" will be understood when such experiences as the following are recounted:

Mozan Ih lived towards the end of the Southern Sung Dynasty in the thirteenth century, which was about the time when the study of Zen through the koan methodology had already become a fixed programme for all Zen devotees in China. The case of Mozan may be regarded as especially strong in bringing out the psychological aspect of the koan exercise. The following[1] is quoted from Shuko's work on *Whipping Progress through the Frontier-gates of Zen*:

"It was when I was twenty years old that I became

[1] Freely translated.

acquainted with 'The Matter', (i.e. with Zen). I saw
seventeen or eighteen Zen masters before I was thirty-two
and asked them how to make progress in Zen, but nothing
much was gained. Finally I came to Kwanzan, the old
master, who told me to see the *Mu*. He then gave me the
following advice: 'Throughout the twelve periods of day,
be like a cat trying to catch a rat, or like a hen holding
her chicks under the wings; be ever on the alert, and do
not let any intermission take place. While you have not
yet attained a penetrating insight, be like a rat gnawing
at the coffin; do not allow yourself to be sidetracked. If
you keep on like this, the time will certainly be yours when
you will be awakened (to the meaning of the koan).'

"Thereupon I applied myself most assiduously to the
koan day and night. Eighteen days passed; while sipping
tea I abruptly came upon the meaning of 'the Buddha
holding up the flowers and Kashyapa smiling'. Unable
to restrain my joy, I sought interviews with three or four
masters, wishing to have them certify my understanding.
But they did not say a word, except one who told me to
stamp them all with one stamp known as *sagara-mudra-
samadhi* ('ocean-stamp meditation'), and not to be
bothered about anything else. Believing this, I passed two
years.

"In June, in the fifth year of Ching-ting (1264), I was in
the district of Chung-Ching, in the province of Ssu-
Chuan, where, suffering a severe case of diarrhoea, I had
to stool more than one hundred times in twenty-four hours.
I was utterly exhausted, and at this most critical moment
the *sagara-mudra-samadhi* was of no use whatever, nor was
the knowledge which I had acquired of any avail. My
mouth refused to utter a sound, my body to move an
inch; just waiting for deaht I laid myself down. All the
karma-conditioned scenes of my past life simultaneously
presented themselves before my mental eyes, and I was
horror-stricken and underwent an unspeakable suffering.

"Finally I made up my mind to overcome all this. I
told people about me how to arrange affairs after my
death. The cushions were laid thick, a stick of incense

was lighted, and slowly rising from bed I took my seat. I silently offered prayers to the Triple Treasure and to the gods, and repented all my deeds which were not in accord with the Buddhist teaching. My prayer was this: 'If death is inevitable may I be conceived, by virtue of the Prajna power, in the womb of a pure-hearted woman and join the Buddhist Brotherhood in my early youth. If I should recover, however, I will give up my worldly life and become a monk, and attaining enlightenment within a short period, instruct the young as extensively as I can in the Dharma.'

"The prayer finished, I applied myself to the Mu, deeply reflecting within myself. After some little while I felt my viscera turning in convolution three or four times, but I paid no attention. Some time passed, and my eyelids were steadied; some more time, and I was not aware of my own bodily existence; my koan alone occupied the whole field of consciousness. Towards the evening I rose from my seat feeling very much better. I sat again, keeping up this posture till midnight, even to early hours of the morning, when I found all my sickness gone, with mind and body light and easy.

"In August I went to Kiang-ling and had my head shaved. A year elapsed before I began my Zen pilgrimage. While cooking rice on the way I discovered that the exercising in koan should be one uninterrupted activity. I joined the Brotherhood at Huan-lung. When sleepiness first attacked me, I resisted it without very much striving. When it came over me for a second time, I managed again to drive it away without much difficulty. But when it crept in for a third time, I left my seat and came down on the ground, where I performed my bowings. Then I came back to the cushion and continued my meditation.

"When the regulation time for general sleeping was announced I gave myself up to a short sound sleep. First I used a pillow and later substituted the arm. Afterwards, however, I did not allow myself to lie down for a sleep. Two or three nights passed; I felt tired and exhausted day and night, I was not at all conscious of my legs touching the earth. I then suddenly felt as if dark clouds were dispersing before my eyes, and my whole body freshened up as if coming out of a bath. I felt generally light and enlivened, whereas the 'doubt-mass' was growing strong, for it kept itself before my consciousness on its own accord, without my making special efforts to do so. All the defiling passions kept themselves away from my mind. My senses were as immaculate as a silver vessel filled with snow, as austere as the autumn atmosphere. But I reflected that however happily I might be advancing in my exercise, I did not seem to be making any decisive turn. So I decided to leave this place and go to the Che district.

"On the way I had to suffer many hardships which proved unfavourable to my progress. I was finally settled under the tutorship of the master Shoten Kosen. I then vowed not to leave the monastery until I had something of enlightenment (*satori*). In a little over one month's exercise I regained the former stage of concentration, when I was troubled with sores covering the entire body. I paid no attention to it. Not caring for aught that might happen to me, I pressed on with my koan exercise, and made quite a considerable advance in it, thus proving myself to be equal to an unfavourable bodily condition. When I was invited out for a dinner I never lost sight, while walking, of the koan which occupied my mind. I did not notice the house of my host and passed by further on. This showed that I could keep up with the koan even while engaged in bodily work.

"At this stage my mind was like a moon casting its shadow on the waters; however tempestuous the waves might be, or however swiftly the rapids might be running, the reflection was not disturbed, nor was it obliterated.

"On the sixth of March, while sitting in meditation with the *Mu*, the head monk entered the Hall and, trying to burn incense before the shrine, happened to drop the incense case on the floor, which made a sound. Abruptly I was awakened from the meditation, became cognizant of the Self and caught Joshu the old master.

"My impromptu verse ran thus:

As it chanced, the road has come to a terminus,
Step on them, the waves are water itself.
The old master Joshu stands towering above others,
But his real features are just this.

"During the autumn I was in Lin-an, where I interviewed such great masters as Setsugan, Taiko, Sekiko, Kyoshu. The last advised me to see Kwanzan. When I saw him, he asked: 'The light serenely bright illuminates all the worlds as numerous as sands of the Ganga: Are these not the words of Chosetsu, the literati?' No sooner had I tried to open my mouth than he struck me and chased me out. After that I lost appetite for food and drink, and had no will for purposeful work (for the doubt raised by Kwanzan's treatment occupied my entire consciousness). I thus passed six months.

"Next spring I happened, while coming back from a trip out of the city, to climb the stone steps, when I suddenly felt my inside obstructions melt away like ice, and was no more conscious of my body treading the ground. I then interviewed Kwanzan, who asked me the same question as before, and I overturned his chair. He now let me go over several koan which had hitherto resisted solution because of their intricacies, and I passed them one after another, leaving not a shadow of doubt about them.

"I can tell you this now, O Brethren: If I were not taken ill at Chung-Ching I might have passed a useless life. The important point is to seek out a master with the right understanding. For this reason the old masters are devoted most assiduously day and night to the adjustment of their innermost difficulties. Be ever studious, O Brethren, and always on the alert in your pursuit of 'This Business'."

The following case is taken from a book entitled *Keikyaku sodan*[1] containing accounts of Hakuin's disciples. Sui-o was one of the chief disciples of Hakuin. He had

[1] *Stories of the Thorns and Brambles*, 1829.

among his followers a monk from Ryukyu, to whom the koan of "one hand" was given. The monk spent three years on it but failed to make any headway. When time limits he set for himself reached the end, he came to Sui-o and said: "I come from a distant island of Ryūkyū far out in the ocean, and my object of being here with you is to have an insight into the Right Dharma. Unfortunately, my past karma is heavy yet, and I have not attained my objective. I deeply lament returning to my native island with the same old face." Sui-o consoled him, saying: "Don't be discouraged. Delay your departure for a week and see if you cannot get settled with your koan."

The monk retired; seven days of meditation passed; nothing happened. He came back to Sui-o and reported. The master said, "Try another week and see if you cannot clear up the matter." The monk followed his advice, but with no result, as before. Sui-o was patient, in spite of his being noted for the opposite quality, and told the monk, "There are many Zen students who were able to come to satori within three weeks; try your luck for a third week." When this was over, he appeared before Sui-o covered with tears, and said, "I have not gained anything yet, what shall I do?" Sui-o said, "Go and devote five days this time to the koan."

After five days he had to make the same report as before. Sui-o now advised him: "When you go on like this, you can never come to a realization. You must drive at the matter with all the energy in your possession, and if you still cannot come to a solution, what is the use of living any longer?" This incited the monk. He now decided to attack the koan even at the risk of his life. At the end of the three days he finally succeeded in overcoming all the difficulties which impeded his progress. He came to Sui-o, this time in quite a different frame of mind, and the master was pleased to give his sanction. This incident appropriately illustrates the ancient saying:

When not spurred, no awakening;
When not cornered, no opening through.

Records of Hakuin and Bukko the National Teacher are given in my *Essays in Zen Buddhism*, Series One, 1927. Both of them exercised themselves in the koan "*Mu*", and came to a satori only after years of wrestling with it.

From these accounts, readers can understand what I mean by the "psychological aspect of satori". This aspect was hardly noticeable among Zen followers prior to the advent of the Koan system. Whatever their efforts in trying to solve the great problems of life, they have been on the intellectual side of satori. They have not had any one particular theme, later known as koan, for the solution of which all their mental powers were concentrated. This can be seen from the mondo which they had with their masters. The mondo are on various subjects, of various kinds. "What is the meaning of Bodhi-Dharma's coming from the West?" "What is the essence of Buddhism?" "What is the Buddha?" "Am I endowed with the Buddha-nature?" "What is Enlightenment?" "Who is the original person?" "How shall I escape from birth-and-death?"—some such questions were asked of the master, and the master would give them most unexpected answers which completely baffled the monks, but this very unexpectedness gave a new orientation to their inquiries, and it even opened their eyes to the truth they had been seeking.

A monk asked, "I have a doubt which the master would kindly settle." But even before the master knew what kind of doubt it was, the doubter was brought before the congregation, to whom the master declared, "O monks, here is the one who has a doubt." The master left him to his own devices to settle the doubt, whatever it was.

All this changed with the coming of the koan. According to the advocates of the koan, whatever kind of doubts, and however many of them you may have, they all resolve into one doubt. Concentrate this one doubt on the koan, and when this is solved all your doubts, of whatever sort, will dissolve, and your intellectual suspense will come to an end.

Says Daiye: "As long as your doubts as to the whence and whither of life find no solution, thoughts on birth-and-death get intercrossed and hopelessly entangled in your mind, and at this very point of intercrossing you set this koan and see what it means: A monk asked Joshu, 'Is the Buddha-nature present in the dog?' Joshu replied, 'No (*mu*).' Gathering up all the doubt-threads of entanglement, transfer them on to the koan, and you will discover that all the turmoils subside and the suspension of a doubting mind will begin to settle, but not quite fully. Direct your koan against this half-settling mind, and push it to the furthest limits. When the time comes, the limits will vanish by themselves, and you will find that all that you formerly thought defiled was simply due to a wrong discrimination, etc."[1]

We can now see that the koan is a kind of pointer to those who have lost their way. When the mind is harassed with every sort of doubt, anxiety, and vacillation, from whatever sources these may arise, intellectual or emotional, the koan will lift it up and direct it towards its solution as the thing most urgently needed at the moment. For this the Zen student is logically called upon to have a most definite faith in the efficacy of the koan to solve all his troubles, and also in the Zen tradition which, according to the master, has originated from the Mind itself, that is, the Buddha-nature, which is the absolute source of all things. Those who lack this faith, which is claimed by Buddhists to be innate in us all—and to deny it is suicidal—cannot hope to progress in the mastery of the koan. Such a one will go back to the old method, natural, self-dependent, and painstaking, of reaching a final solution.

---

[1] An abstract from Daiye's letter to Myomyo Koji. *The Daiye Goroku*, Vol. XXIII.

V

According to Daiye, a most determined mind is needed if a man wishes to attain the stage of Buddhahood, wherein he has satori and realizes a perfect state of emancipation and the feeling of absolute rest; and, further, he says that when you have no determined mind to experience the opening of your spiritual eye in this life, you can never awaken a most determined faith. But in my view the faith comes first, and a most determined mind is awakened through the working of faith, but the latter generally lies hidden in the depths of unconsciousness, and for that reason its presence in the mind is not recognized. You are apt to think that it is by reason of a determined mind to attain enlightenment that faith asserts itself. But if it were not already there in your unconscious it would never come to the surface and demand your recognition; not only that, your very determination would never be made, and it would never, therefore, be brought to fulfilment.

Faith is then more fundamental than the determined will which is psychologically needed for bringing up the hidden treasure to a fuller consciousness.

This emphasis upon the importance of strong-mindedness in the pursuance of Zen has steadily gained force as the koan system became an established method for attaining satori. It is said that disciplining oneself in the way is like making a fire; as you see the smoke rise, make every effort to keep it up and do not suspend your labour until the golden star finally makes it appearance. This is the coming home, i.e. arriving at your destination.

Isan once asked Rai-an: "How are you getting along these days?" "I am attending my cow." "How do you attend to her?" "Each time she gets among the weeds, I pull her out by the nose-ring." Said Isan, "You are a good cowherd indeed." In this way the Zen student is persuaded to keep up his vigilance over the mind so as not to let it go away from the right track. He is to be an "iron fellow". Once his mind is made up, he is to go ahead regardless of good or evil, right or wrong, until he finally puts his fingers right on supreme enlightenment (*sambodhi*), which is satori.

Faith is fundamental but lies dormant, as it were, deep in our consciousness, and is awakened by a man of strong determination. This determination is possible only when faith begins to make itself known to him. If there is no faith from the first in his inner being, there will be no mind to make a determination. This faith, however, is not the one to which we ordinarily refer, because it has no object to which it applies itself, nor has it any subject from which it goes out to something other than itself. This fundamental faith is thus subjectless as well as objectless, and as there is in it neither subject nor object, it is not any particular psychological event, nor is it a specifically definable concept; nor is it on that account a mere nothing.

Daiye says in his letter to Muso-koji, one of his lay-disciples: "The superior person's understanding of the Way is like stamping emptiness of space with a stamp; the middling person's understanding is like stamping water with a stamp; and the inferior person's understanding is like stamping the mud with a stamp. The stamp itself makes no difference whether it stamps space or water or mud. The difference arises from the different qualities of personality. If you wish at this very moment to enter upon the Way, come to me with the stamp together with everything else all broken to pieces,[1] and thus you will see me."

---

[1] Daiye in another refers to the smashing of "the mirror":

"The Buddha is the mirror of the unenlightened and even the unenlightened are the mirror of the Buddha. When the unenlightened go astray, the images of birth-and-death and their defilements are reflected in their entirety in the Buddha-mirror. When the unenlightened are all of a sudden awakened to a state of enlightenment, the Buddha-image of genuine purity and mysterious brightness which transcends birth-and-death is reflected even in the mirror of the unenlightened.

"The Buddha, however, knows from the first neither birth nor death, neither ignorance nor enlightenment, nor has he any mirror, nor is there any image which reflects itself in it. Only because of the unenlightened

This stamp of faith we commonly put on the mud of objectivity, expecting to see its mark concretely defined. But the faith of Zen is even less than stamping on the emptiness of space, for Zen demands that the stamp itself be broken to pieces, which is beyond the ken of visibility. But that it is not a stamp of sheer negation is inferred from the following passage, again from Daiye's letter, this time to Myosho-koji, where the statement concerns itself with concrete images containing nothing suggestive of absolute annihilation, though it is full of "absurdities" from the relative point of view. The story runs thus:

A monk asked Joshu, "Is it possible that the cypress-tree is in possession of the Buddha-nature?" "Yes, it is." "When does it attain Buddhahood?" "Wait until the void falls down on earth," rejoined Joshu. "When does the void fall down on earth?" "Wait until the cypress-tree attains Buddhahood," was Joshu's reply.

On this, Daiye comments: "You do not cherish the thought of the cypress-tree's not attaining Buddhahood, nor of the void's falling down on earth. What then? When the void falls down on earth, the cypress-tree attains Buddhahood; when the cypress-tree attains Buddhahood, the void falls down on earth. This is certain. Please think of it."

---

involved in various (enlightenments, the Buddha) adapting himself to them has devised (various ways of deliverance).

"Now if you wish to do away with the disease of the unenlightened and not to be different from the Buddha and Patriarchs, I request you to come to me with the mirror smashed into pieces, and then I may for your sake make some comments on this matter."

In this connection, Seppo's interviews with Tokusan will be found illuminating:

"Seppo for the sake of 'this matter' went up three times to Tosu and nine times to Tozan, but failed to get it. Later, hearing of Tokusan's missionary activities, he visited him, and asked him one day about the truth of Zen, which had been handed down by successive masters since the coming from the West of Bodhi-Dharma. Said Tokusan, 'Wordiness is not of our school, nor is there any one particular thing that is to be given to others.' Later on, Seppo asked again, 'As regards the matter handed down by successive masters, can I claim something of it too?' Tokusan made no delay in taking up his staff and striking Seppo hard, saying 'What do you say?' This at once opened Seppo's eyes to the truth of Zen."

What is to be noted here as everywhere else in the Zen teaching is that it uses concrete expressions familiar to our daily life, yet in such a way as to contradict our common-sense experience in a world of realities, as if we were living in a realm of topsyturvydom. This usage in Zen, however, demonstrates most effectively that Zen, in spite of its appearing to be altogether nihilistic, is endeavouring to show us a world of concrete particulars, which is diametrically opposed to our common-sense world and yet does not deny it. The world of Zen is a reconstruction of the old world from an entirely novel point of view; in this respect Zen is entirely Copernican.

When I say that Zen faith is not a faith in its vulgar connotation, but one in which there is neither subject nor object, i.e. a faith that is no-faith, the idea is that there is a real world superimposed, as it were, upon our world of sense-intellect, and that when this is understood, the latter as it is becomes a real world, or we can say that we create a new world. This means that in Zen faith is ever creative, whereby we live a new life every moment, that there is nothing old and repeated in the world of Zen, and consequently that Zen is not dominated by empty concepts and abstractions and generalities.

Kisu Shikigen was once asked by a monk, "What is the Buddha?" "If I tell you, you won't believe." "Why should I not believe your word of truth?" Kisu said, "You are he." Hearing this, the monk reflected within himself for a little while and finally said, "If I am the Buddha himself, how should I take care of (myself)?" "If there is even a particle of dust in the eye, flowers are seen dancing in the air." This warning on the part of Kisu at once awakened the monk's mind to a state of satori.

Daiye remarks on this incident: "The monk in the beginning had no definite faith in himself; even when he heard Kisu's direct pointing to the truth he was still in doubt as to his being the Buddha himself, and expressed his desire to be informed in regard to the taking care of himself. When this was assured he thought he could bring himself to the belief that he and the Buddha were identical. Kisu was kind-hearted, and directly struck with his royal Vajra-sword exactly at the spot where the monk was wavering and about to contradict himself. The monk was standing on one leg at the edge of the precipice ten thousand feet high; swept off by one stroke of Kisu's sword he lost his wavering balance, and understood how to throw himself down over the precipice."

From the logical point of view, the koan helps to settle all kinds of doubt about the nature and destiny of man, and other religious and philosophical problems, concentrating them on the one doubt which the koan evokes. The koan itself has no magical power; it is no more than "a piece of brick", as they say, to knock at the door, or a finger to point at the moon. The main thing is to have satori by means of a koan. Therefore, the two are most intimately related. Satori as an experience is psychological, and the koan, therefore, has its own psychological aspect. The koan, as it is, is illogically formulated, and as far as its solution is concerned is purely on the plane of logic, though this logic is not what most of us ordinarily understand.

When you understand that a fan is a fan when it is no-fan, this understanding is intellectual, or rather super-intellectual, and has nothing to do with one's psychology. But as every understanding, however pure or abstract, is backed by experience, it is to that extent psychological. Satori has its own psychology as well as its own logic. We must not, however, suppose that the mere combination of psychology and logic in an experience constitutes satori, for in satori there must be something coming from the spiritual plane of life, and this which may be called spiritual or supernatural or super-rational—is Zen.

The psychology of satori is concerned with the affective aspect of consciousness when the koan is to be attacked with what Daiye called "a determined mind". Sustained efforts are required in the solution of a koan, and these efforts are strongly volitional. What supports and sustains the intellectual curiosity excited by it is a resolute will. This is requisite in everything a man may attempt, and especially it holds true in the case of koan solution. The master is there to exhaust your energy and test what progress you make; he is ever after you. As long as you have something to say in words, your encounter with the master may not be very trying. But the time will come when you have nothing to say and yet you are requested to interview him, sometimes frequently, and you do not know what to do. If you are sitting in the Zendo (meditation hall) together with other seekers of truth, a senior supervisor will be prodding you all the time to see the master if you fail to report to him at the proper time.

This "prodding" may be regarded as irrelevant, because the koan solution is not a matter concerning others but your own affair, and you volunteered to do the work for your own sake and by your own efforts. The fact is, however, that all these irrelevant artificialities help the student to arrive at a stage of satori experience. "A determined mind" is often thus efficiently cultivated to sustain the weaker-minded not to give up their first intention. There is something in our mental constitution which prepares itself for the satori condition by being artificially reconstructed or stimulated.

"Plodding" or no "prodding", the main idea is to bring the mind to a state of concentration, to a state of the highest possible tension so as to leave for the mind just two courses to pursue; either to break down and possibly go out of mind, or to go beyond the limits and open up an entirely new vista, which is satori. When one has no steadiness of purpose, clearly defined and consciously presented to the mind at the beginning of the koan exercise, the psychological tension may result in an unhappy outbreak, frequently tinged with a sense of pride even when it happily culminates in satori. This going off the right track may come from the patient's being neurotically predisposed. Ordinarily, things go on as they ought to, and the koan brings the result as intended, or rather it comes to its natural and logical conclusion, satisfactory in every way as far as satori is concerned, though "natural and logical" here is to be understood as synonymous with "super-natural and super-logical".

The psychological importance of "a determined mind" or a resolute will, which never rests until the goal is reached, is thus evident; this corresponds to the logical importance of pursuing the line of a doubt to its furthest end. When logic fails to reach an end, as it must because of its inherent impotence as the instrument of giving satisfaction to our spiritual unrest, we are made to stand at the edge of a precipice where there is no turning back, for we have logically followed step by step and have now come to the limits of logic, beyond which there is a bottomless, gaping abyss.

The determined mind still persists, and demands that we leap over the precipice, no matter what happens. The mind as a logical instrument gives way to the mind as embodying the spirit. This is the walking on "the white road" under the beckoning of Amida on the other side of the stream of fire and water. This is being embraced by the grace of God who now reveals himself through the opening of the darkest clouds of naturalism. The event is variously designated by the different religious systems as enlightenment, salvation, emancipation, regeneration, the birth in the Pure Land, etc. Satori is Zen's terminology. All things in Zen start from it and end in "forgetting" it. A satori that remains a satori all the time is no satori; it is known as one that smells too much of itself. It has to lose itself in order to be itself. Such is satori.

Satori itself has nothing to do with psychology or with logic, but when the koan system developed it naturally came to be treated from the psychological aspect. While satori in the koan system more or less lost its characteristic as something spontaneously rising from the inmost depths of the unconscious, it now began to be regarded artificially, humanly, psychologically forced to reveal itself to the consciousness of the individual concerned. The importance of psychology is keenly felt here, and the masters insist on the necessity of a steady, determined, sincere mind, without which the iron wall of the koan will never yield to the attack of the Zen student.

Let me quote Daiye again in this connection, for it was after Yengo and Daiye, both of the Sung Dynasty, that the koan system gradually came to assume importance in the mastery of Zen, and it was indeed Daiye himself who was identified as the originator of the koan against the so-called "silent contemplation" school of Wanshi (1091–1157).

Daiye strongly maintained that the silent contemplation advocated by Wanshi and his pupils was liable to lead one's mind to the practice of emptying itself of all its contents, and that the outcome was killing Zen and leaving it cold as stone. Wanshi and his school retorted that the study of Zen by the koan was too artificial and would create in the mind of the student a confused idea whereby he takes the means for the end itself. Whatever this may be, Daiye upheld the importance of a strong will in the study of Zen. The following is an abstract of what he states about the subject in his long letter to Myomyo, one of his lay-disciples:

"If you have already understood what the Mind is, and further wish to realize this 'One Thing', you must first of all erect a strong determined will. In whatever surroundings and relationships, desirable or undesirable, you may find yourself, do not fail to take hold of yourself, to be your own master and watch over yourself lest you be carried away by false views variously promulgated.

"In your daily intercourse with the outside world, be sure all the time to have these two characters, birth-and-death, pasted on the tip of your nose, remembering that all things are transient and subject to constant change.

"It is, again, like a man who is deeply involved in debt. He finds himself unable to meet his obligations when his creditors stand at the doorpost and demand settlement right away. He is worried over it, he is fearful of what will happen to him next, he exhausts all his wits trying to find a way to pay the debts, but he cannot come to any definite conclusion. He is at an impasse.

"If you are able to retain this state of mind all the time (in regard to the solving of the koan), you will somehow come to the way of final settlement. If, however, you halt, wondering whether to believe or not to believe, whether to go ahead or beat retreat, you will never achieve anything. You are worse than an illiterate simpleton in the remotest parts of the country. Why? Because by reason of his utter ignorance he is altogether free from wrong views and misleading notions which will surely prove hindrances (to his realization). He is wise in holding fast single-mindedly to his ignorant ways.

"Says an old wise man: In the pursuance of the ultimate truth, satori is the criterion. Recently there have been a number of Zen masters who do not believe in satori, thinking that it is deceptive and misleading, that it is an artificial construction, the unnecessary setting up of a blockade, that it is altogether of secondary importance. There are indeed a large number of people who, putting on a lion's skin, give out a fox's cry. Those who have not yet opened a Dharma-discerning eye are often deceived by them. For this reason you have to be always on guard and give everything a thorough examination so as not to be led astray."

Koho Gemmyo (–1295), of the Temmoku monastery, harps more or less on the same string with Daiye when he says: "As to this matter (the studying of Zen), the most important thing is to have a steady determined mind. When you have this, you will before long have a genuine doubt rising. When you go on with this doubt, firmly taking hold of your mind, it will occupy the whole field of your consciousness. Without you paying special attention to it, it will always be present. From morning till evening, let the head follow the tail and the tail the head in an unbroken succession until the whole thing assumes one solid indivisible continuum. Shaking will not dislocate it, chasing will not turn it out. How serenely luminous! It is ever present in the mind. This is the time you have made some definite progress in the handling of the koan.

"Still holding fast to the right thought, never slide back, never cherish a divided mind; when you go on like this you will come to the point where you are not conscious of sitting or walking; nor will you be, aware of cold and heat, of hunger and thirst. When this state of mind is realized you are said to have had good tidings of the Home. But still be careful not to give up your firm hold of the situation. Just go on with your steady grip and wait for the time to arrive when satori reveals itself.

"Here, however, is an all-important consideration. You just go on with steady, single-minded pursuit of the koan, and never pay any regard to whatever things may follow or may not. Cherish no expectations, have no self-suggestions; just go on with your koan single-mindedly. As this is a most desirable opportunity for all kinds of evil spirits to work havoc in your mind and wreck all that you have so far achieved, you ought to be on the alert, so as not to deviate from the right course. If you do, the efficient cause of Prajna will forever be lost and the seed of enlightenment will never be able to germinate. Beware of letting the mind wander away from the right course. Be like a spirit who watches over the corpse with singleness of purpose, and you will come to see that the lump of doubt[1] you have been nourishing will all of a sudden

[1] "The lump of doubt" (would it be better to say "the mass of doubt"?) in English may sound strange. The original Chinese is *i tuan tze*, quite expressive of the actual state of mind in which the koan student finds himself when he has pursued it up to a certain stage. It is not an intellectual term but a state of psychological impasse. "Doubt" suggests the former, but what the Zen master has in mind in this case is a kind of mental blockade. The stream of thought is locked up; it does not run on but is frozen and forms a lump. It is in one sense a state of concentration. The entire field of consciousness is now occupied with this "lump". This is the "lump of doubt" as it keeps in check the natural current of ideas ordinarily smoothly flowing. Satori is attained when this blockade is broken through. That is to say, at the very moment when consciousness starts to resume its normal activity, it becomes abruptly aware of this event, and the event at once assumes a significance extending beyond its psychology. The lump is gone, the doubt is exploded, and a new vista of life, hitherto unimagined, opens up.

break up into pieces, at the same time crushing down heaven and earth."

VI

In the pursuit of the koan exercise it is often found that a determined will alone does not achieve the end. In some personalities certain shocks are needed to turn the mind out of a groove. The needed shocks come in a form of intense emotional excitement such as anger, indignation, humiliation, etc. Such passions, when incited to a certain degree of intensity, acquire an extraordinary power to break through the limits of consciousness which we generally set for it. In other words, an intense emotional disturbance often awakens in us a mysterious power of which we have ordinarily been unaware.

Confucius told one of his disciples who complained about his inability to advance in virtue: "You limit yourself; it is not that you are not able to do this, but that you simply do not do it." To break down this barrier of self-imposed limitation it is important, it is indeed necessary, to excite the person by some extraordinary measure. The Zen masters apparently knew this secret of human psychology, and appealed to it on appropriate occasions. Their kicking down or giving blows to the disciple, or some such deeds of obviously unkind nature, are not necessarily meant to work up his emotions of resentment, but we sometimes find the masters making use of this feeling.

Date Jitoku, of the early Meiji era of Japan, was one of the chief retainers of the Lord of Kishu. He once incurred the displeasure of the Lord and was imprisoned in his own house. As he found himself enjoying a forced leisure he took up the study of the Buddhist Tripitaka, which engrossed his attention. When he was released after some years he decided to practise Zen. He was introduced to a Zen master in Kyoto who was noted for his severe treatment of his disciples. Jitoku was given a koan. When he came to the master to present his view, the master did not say a word, but struck him hard on his head. This naturally angered the proud old samurai. He expressed himself to his monk-friend who introduced him to the master: "I belong to the samurai class, and have never been treated so ignominiously even by my lord or by my father. I cannot suffer this indignity. I must have the matter settled with that insolent quack. I will cut his head off and commit *seppuku* myself. It is impossible for my honour to endure this shame. The monk-friend quietly said: "Even if you cut his head off, it will not do any good to either of you. From the first, he has no idea of self; he is doing all for the sake of Zen. Rather see that the striking has something significant about it."

Jitoku shut himself up in his room and meditated on the koan with all the intensity of his mind. After some days the meaning of it dawned on him. He rushed to the master's room, and confessed that if his blow were many times harder the satori would have been far deeper and more penetrating still.

Imagita Kosen (1816–1892) was one of the great Zen masters of modern Japan. He was a Confucian in his younger days, but, not being satisfied with it, he came to Zen and became a Zen monk when he was twenty-five years old. His master was a great disciplinarian and treated Kosen with the utmost severity. One day Kosen was told to serve a soup of *tofu* (bean curd) for the master's visitor. Kosen was not brought up as a good cook and failed to cut the *tofu* properly. This angered the master to a degree of unjustifiable intensity, for he insisted upon expelling Kosen from the monastery for his fault. The punishment was not at all in proportion to the offence, which appears to us outsiders altogether trivial. Kosen apologized for his fault in all humiliation, but the master was unyielding. The novitiate monk did not know what to do and was in a state of utmost dejection. Seeing this, one of his fellow-monks, who was his senior and took much interest in him, interceded on his behalf and finally succeeded in placating the master.

Kosen once, while listening to the master's discourse on a Zen text, thought he had a satori. The passage which struck him ran thus:

> The shadows of the bamboo-leaves are sweeping the steps,
>   but the dust is not stirred at all;
> The reflection of the moon has penetrated the bottom of the stream,
>   but no traces are left on the waves.

This is a noted couplet of seven characters which also once engaged the deep concern of Bukko Kohushi, the founder of Engakuji, Kamakura, the monastery over which Kosen came to preside later.[1]

Daisetsu, the master, however, paid no attention to Kosen's presentation of his view. This heartless rejection caused Kosen to concentrate whatever mental strength or intuitional potentialities he had in the koan. He found himself now in a more desperate situation. He could not find any way to go ahead, nor was there any means to retract from the position he had so far gained. Each time he presented his views to the master, the latter repulsed them unconditionally; not only that, he gave him angry blows.

Kosen was despondent, and lamented the heavy burden of his past karma which retarded his spiritual awakening, but the master never relaxed his acrimony, which almost amounted to a revengeful malignity. Kosen never wavered, however sorrowful he was for his unfortunate condition. He was all the more reverential to the teacher who happened to be ill those days, and did everything within his power as a kind of attendant-nurse to give him comfort and relief.

Kosen grew emaciated, losing appetite for food and looking pale and bloodless. His fellow-monks thought

---

[1] And in which Dr. Suzuki himself later lived.—[Ed.]

he might succumb any day to the ordeal. He himself, however, felt differently, for he was growing surer of his advance in grappling with the situation. One evening he entered into the meditation hall, which was vacant because of the occupants being temporarily on a visit to another monastery where a great memorial gathering for a noted master was taking place.

Kosen spent the whole night deeply absorbed in meditation, quite unaware of the dawn's approaching. He only vaguely heard the board being struck for the morning. He knew that the time was ripening for a dénouement. He doubled his efforts to keep his koan before him. He did not leave the hall all day, forgetting meal-times. Towards the evening he abruptly realized that he was in a state most exquisitely pleasant; his senses gained an extra clarity with no differentiation between them. This did not last long, for now he felt his inside extraordinarily clear and broadened out, and his spiritual eye was opened; he heard a voice, saw a vision, both of which were not those of the earth. As if tasting nectar, he knew what was what. All doubts, all the scholarship which had obscured his view, were all wiped off, and he burst out into an exclamation: "How wonderful, how wonderful! I have my satori now, which turns all holy books into a candlelight in the sun."

There are many such instances recorded in the annals of Zen. A monk who was confident of his right under-standing of a koan was severely criticized by his master and forced out of the door. So overworked was he with feelings of shame and indignation that he sat the night out meditating on the problem. It was a hot summer night, and he was thinly dressed. The mosquitoes were fierce. He fought with their ravenous appetite, holding the koan at the centre of consciousness. This went on till the morning dawned, when the meaning of the master's "ill" treatment was understood. When he rose from his meditation, the mosquitoes, roundly distended with blood, it is said, rolled down his body like dewdrops.

Another monk, of the Sung Dynasty, visited a master who was specially noted for his rough handling of pupils. They dared not approach him, and the monastery was left almost deserted. But this particular monk did not mind the master's ill-temper and stuck to him even when he threw a pailful of water into the meditation hall in the middle of the coldest winter month. He shivered but kept on with his meditation. This dogged persistence on the part of the monk finally softened the hardness of the master's heart, and it is said that he consented to take the monk as his pupil.

Shoju Ronin's treatment of Hakuin is well known. The latter was kicked off the porch one rainy summer evening when the master grew impatient with Hakuin's insistence on the correctness of his own understanding. The harshness was probably necessary to get Hakuin out of the track in which he was helplessly grovelling. On such occasions no intellectual arguments could rescue him, no verbal persuasion was of any avail unless something abruptly started from the inside and swept aside at one stroke all that had been nestling comfortably in his mind. This abrupt awakening was possible only under the impact of a strong emotional disturbance. When Hakuin was out begging in the village he did not notice at one house an old woman who refused to give him anything; he just stood there as if pressing her to a charitable deed, which exasperated her to such an extent that she struck him with a broom. Hakuin was rudely knocked down, but this catastrophe awakened from the depths of his unconsciousness an understanding beyond logical comprehension.

VII

As far as the psychological aspect of satori is concerned, it is evident that the system requires that the student's mental powers be raised to their highest possible pitch. This means that the koan brings him to the uppermost end of his existentiality, which is at the same time its lowermost end. When either end is reached, nothing is left for him but to give up all that he has dearly cherished as his own, to annihilate himself completely, as in fact he has nothing left to himself. This is the time that as Adam he dies to himself. He now faces utter blankness; he knows of nothing confronting him, he simply goes on although he is quite aware of his leaping over the precipice. And finally he leaps, and lo, he finds himself, he finds that he is no more, no less than his old self, he finds that he is in the same old world with Mount Fuji snow-covered and the Pacific Ocean washing the Tago-no-ura beach as in the days of Yamabe no Akahito, the poet.

Psychology recedes and vanishes altogether, for metaphysics has now taken its place, metaphysics not based upon the reason but that which grows out of a man's inner being. The latter was a closed book for him; he had no idea of what it could be; but now that it reveals itself to him he feels as if he were back in his own home. There is nothing strange here—he finds everything just as it was before—the misty rain on Mount Lu and the surging waves in the Che-kiang.

Whatever psychological process a man may pass through in the koan exercise, its significance is not in the psychology but in its final "metaphysical" understanding. The psychology is not to be slighted, it has a value in its own way, but this is not where it has its position in the mastery of Zen. If it did not open the secret door of satori for its devotees, it would be an unnecessary, indeed cumbersome, appendage for Zen, as it is liable to involve them in inextricable meshes. The koan must find its justification in waking them to a state of genuine satori and not a mere psychological condition. Our satori must have a new fresh outlook on the world and humanity; it must prove itself useful and valuable in our daily life not only as an individual but as a world citizen, as a member in a system of infinite complexities which contains every conceivable existence, non-sentient as well as sentient.

The reason why the old masters of Zen often make

references to "the right course" in the pursuance of the koan exercise is because its devotees are apt to go astray in various ways, psychologically, logically, and spiritually. They must be guided carefully by a capable experienced teacher who knows perfectly well how to train his pupils. The koan thus frequently proves a dangerous and probably useless instrument in the study of Zen.

Bankei, one of the greatest Zen masters of modern Japan, strenuously opposed the koan method and called it down as an artificial device. In this he was like followers of the Soto school, but unlike the latter he did not advocate "silent contemplation", the practice of which must have appeared to him just as artificial as the koan method. Bankei's teaching centred in the Unborn or Uncreate, and he told his followers to live by the Unborn with which we are all endowed as we come into this world. The Unborn is our own being as we have it even prior to the world itself; in other words, it is God before he came to be cognizant of himself. It is the Unconscious, but it does not remain so. If it did, it would be non-existent. The Unborn knows itself and is responsive. The koan works in most cases to put a check to the spontaneous operation of the Unborn. The following sermon[1] or mondo of Bankei illustrates the point:

Someone asked Bankei: "According to your teaching of the Unborn, you tell us to remain with it just as we are, but this seems to be a doctrine of indifference.[2] Am I right?" Bankei said, "While you are thus innocently talking to me and listening to my words, suppose someone unexpectedly applied a fire to your back, would you feel the heat or not?" "I should certainly feel it." "If so, you are not indifferent. When you feel the heat, how can you be indifferent? As you are not indifferent, you discriminate between heat and cold, without specifically making up

---

[1] Another of his sermons is quoted elsewhere in connection with various approaches that people make to Zen.

[2] Indifference (avyakrita) is a technical term with Buddhism. When a thing is neither good nor bad, it is said to be indifferent. It means therefore also "insensible", "anaesthetic", "lack of nervous system", "devoid of intelligence", or "a state of undifferentiation and indetermination".

your mind to do so. Further, when you ask about your being right in regard to your understanding, you cannot be said to be indifferent. As you are not indifferent, you come to me of your own free will and express your desire to be enlightened upon the subject. This conclusively shows that the Buddha-mind (i.e. the Unborn) is intelligent, knowing, full of wisdom, and not indifferent (i.e. not insensible and unintelligent). You cannot even for a moment be indifferent. When have you ever been indifferent?"

In another place Bankei teaches: "Your inborn mind is the Buddha-mind itself which knows neither birth nor death. To prove this, consider the fact that when you see things you see them all at once, and when you hear sounds you at once perceive them and can say, this is a bird singing, that is the temple bell. You don't have to reflect about them even for a moment. From morning till night we attend to our business without giving a moment's thought to it, but most people think that this living is carried on by calculation and discrimination.

That is a great mistake. The Unborn is working in us. The Buddha-mind and our mind are not two. Those who strive after satori, or attempt to discover the self-mind, and exert themselves with this in view are committing a great mistake.[1] That the mind is of birth-and-death is well known to anybody who has the slightest knowledge of the *Shingyo* (*Hridaya-Sutra*), but they have not yet sounded the source of the Unborn; they endeavour to reach it by means of discrimination and calculation, thinking this to be the way to Buddhahood. As soon as an attempt is made to realize the Way, to attain Buddhahood, you deviate from the Unborn and lose sight of what is inborn in you. This (inborn) Mind does not say, "I am bright" or "I am dark", it remains to be itself as it is born in you. To try to bring it out into a state of satori is of secondary importance.

You are primarily Buddhas; you are not going to be Buddhas for the first time. There is not an iota of a thing

[1] This evidently refers to devotees of the koan exercise.

to be called error[1] in your inborn mind, from which, let me assure you, not an erring thought ever rises. Clenching your fists firmly, you may run a race—this too is your Unborn. If you have the least desire to be something better than you actually are, if you hurry up to the slightest degree in search of something, you are already going against the Unborn. Your inborn mind is absolutely free from joy as well as anger; there is the Buddha-mind alone, of transcendental intelligence, illuminating all things. Firmly believing in this, have no attachment in your daily life—this is known as a believing heart.[2]

That Bankei's teaching of the Unborn or the Inborn is not the philosophy of instinct for the unconscious has been elsewhere touched upon. If the Unborn is the unconscious, it must be understood not in its psychological sense but in the metaphysical, or ontological, or cosmic sense. The Unborn is not a blind force, nor is it an irrational impulse or mere *élan vital*. According to Bankei, it is intelligent beyond logical calculation, it indiscriminatingly discriminates, it is the principle of order we might say, which directs the intellect to work in the world of practical affairs.

But we must remember that Zen masters, including Bankei, Hakuin, Rinzai, Yakusan and Joshu are not philosophers; they are most practical radical empiricists wanting us to personally confront the Unborn and to live it instead of discoursing on it, or about it. Therefore, when they bring it out on the rational plane their expressions may not be in accordance with rules of logic or dialectic; all they want is to be a guide for us, as the one who has empirically trodden the field of the Unborn.

In concluding this chapter, let me quote another mondo of Bankei and his inquirer on "great doubt". A monk asked: "According to an ancient saying, great doubt yields great understanding (satori), but you are not

---

[1] *Mayoi* in Japanese stands against satori. What is not satori is *mayoi* which literally means "to get lost", "to go astray", "to roam around off the right track".

[2] These quotations are from *Life and Sermons of Bankei Zenshi*, compiled by D. T. Suzuki, 1941.

an advocator of 'great doubt'. Pray tell me why." This question on the part of Bankei's disciple shows that in his day too there must have been a party of koan devotees who talked much about arousing "great doubt" or "lump of doubt", or "mass of doubt", to which reference was made elsewhere, as needed for solving the koan. Bankei did not like this way of studying Zen. He knew there was too much of artifice in the exercise, which was not motivated by the inner need. He thus evidently opposed the koan methodology which tries to create "great doubt" mechanically, as it were. Said Bankei:

"You aroused great doubt in this way: When Nangaku came to the Sixth Patriarch the latter asked, What is this that thus comes here? Nangaku, questioned thus, did not know how to answer. He cherished the doubt for eight years and finally found out: 'When you try to say, this is it, you miss it altogether.' You have genuinely here a case of great doubt and great understanding (satori). It is like a Buddhist priest misplacing his only *kesa* (a ceremonial robe), which he fails to locate in spite of his most anxious hunting. He cannot even for a moment give up the thought of the lost article. This is a doubt genuinely aroused. People of these days try to cherish doubt merely because the old master had it. This is no more than a make-believe; it is like searching after a thing which one has never lost."

Bankei attacks the most vulnerable spot in the koan system. For one thing the koan works on one's psychology and attempts to create a subjective attitude corresponding to that of the genuine philosophically-disposed or religiously-directed mind. The latter has a strong inner prompting, while the former is only desirous of following him. The imitator is not lacking in the inner needs as is demonstrated by the desire to follow Zen; all that such persons need is to be helped by some external means.

No doubt the koan fulfils this office when the discipline is properly guided by an experienced master. Thus properly guided, the imitator may some day become genuine. But there is one thing which requires a full recognition on the part of every koan devotee: This is to remember that each koan is an expression of the Great Intelligence (*mahaprajna*) and that every such expression gains significance only when it is associated with the Great Compassion (*mahakaruna*).

THE END

INDEX